Animals' Petition to God

Animals' Petition to God

Prabhudan Biswasi

ISPCK
Impacting Communities since 1710

2011

Animals' Petition to God - Published by the Rev. Dr. Ashish Amos of Indian Society for Promoting Christian Knowledge (ISPCK), Post Box 1585, 1654, Madarsa Road, Kashmere Gate, Delhi-110006 .

ISBN: 978-81-8465-137-9

Laser typeset by

ISPCK, Post Box 1585, 1654, Madarsa Road, Kashmere Gate, Delhi-110006 • *Tel:* 23866323

e-mail: ashish@ispck.org.in • ella@ispck.org.in
website: www.ispck.org.in

My God,
You are the omniscient
Creator and Liberator.
Kindly help me accomplish
this task of mine.

Contents

Preface

Great personalities of the world, such as Ashoka, Abraham Lincoln, Mahatma Gandhi and Mother Teresa, were able to win the hearts and minds of the people because they were committed to promoting peace, justice, liberty and prosperity. These great men and women struggled a lot to bring about changes in the people—to develop capable leaders—and their environment.

Crime and corruption are now rampant in society. So developing good people is a major need of the hour. Our world would be a better place to live in if it is run by honest and efficient people, if good and honest people constitute the majority of the world population. But how can we realise this dream—that is the question. Strange as it may appear, I have resorted to an unusual way of solving this problem: I have tried to realise this long-cherished dream with the help of some animals. The book, *Animal's Petition to God*, brings to light these animals in an interesting way.

But first let us take a look at the salient features of this book.

- Attempts at revealing God the Creator based on the major religions of the world

- Attempts at presenting the first man based on major religious beliefs

- Promotion of compassion, peace, prosperity and progress

- Society and social transformations

- Presentation of full and rich men on the world stage

- Attempts at producing good people in today's world

Prabhudan Biswasi

Introduction

Indifference, selfishness and despair plague our world. Corruption, lawlessness, murder, rape, environment degradation and pollution are making our lives more and more miserable. Socrates always gave a lot of importance to the goodness of the people. He said that change in the old order of society can be brought about only by good people.

The world we live in is a beautiful place. We share the world with many species of animals. Humans are superior to animals in many respects, as they have four virtues: knowledge, wisdom, conscience and freedom. Man is expected to use these virtues in constructive ways to build up a better world. But on account of evil forces and selfish desires man has used these qualities in destructive ways. Freedom is often misused. This is the reason why there is so much chaos and confusion in the world. So God punishes man by sending terrible diseases, pestilence, famine, etc.

Although we have made rapid progress in science, medicine and technology, we have not been able to successfully deal with most of the evils in today's world. We need to make a concerted effort to root out corruption at all levels; we must fight against inequality, marginalisation and poverty. The poisons of selfishness, ignorance, callousness, anger, greed and hate must be destroyed so that our world becomes a better place to live in.

CHAPTER I

The Petition

Yes, there are many good people on earth. Once, we were going by bus along with a stranger. In the course of conversation, the gentleman said that there was no scarcity of good people in society. A great many of such highly educated and cultured men and women of different parts of the world could foresee the tragic end of humanity and the dire need of goodness on earth. They rose to be most practical in their thoughts and actions. At this critical hour we published an article relating to the human problem in a fitting manner. We invited the addresses of the persons who were interested in social development. In a few days, we could procure the addresses of such persons. Now we let them know the time and place of the meeting. The central place of the world, somewhere in the Middle East, was the venue. Many good people including eminent scholars and social workers gathered there. We started the meeting with great pleasure and enthusiasm. Some members put forth the present problems in the meeting in a customary manner inviting suggestions and solutions. But the tone and tune and the traditional business of the meeting could not draw the attention of the members. Now as many as seven ladies representing different parts of the world gave stirring speeches, which moved the entire house. They proposed that twelve persons, including seven writers, be selected to petition God with humble prayer to grant all the animals, birds and reptiles the four virtues—knowledge, wisdom, conscience and freedom—already granted to humans. The proposal was unanimously accepted. The petitioners designed the petition; the wording of which ran thus: "Our Merciful, Beneficent, Omnipotent, Just and Beloved God, we thank you that you have created us. The greatest gift that you have given to us is life itself. You reveal yourself to us. Your incomparable love to humanity is unforgettable. We live by your grace. You are the best provider. Without you we cannot live in this world even for a moment. You can be directly approached at any time. You are interested in the personal details of our individual life. You want that we should have purity and holiness. But we did not listen to your loving words and went astray. This is sin. This is the reason why there are troubles everywhere in this world. Human beings have become so bad that they are always going against you and their fellowmen. You, as an Omniscient God, know all these things and at the same time you want us to go back to you. But the influence of our temporal world, our selfish desires and the evil forces do not permit us to be good and listen to your call. This is the root cause of all troubles in our society.

"But the animals are better than human beings in many respects. They do not kill or harm their fellow animals. But we do. Therefore, sometimes, we feel that brutality is much better than rationality because the man, who possesses rationality, is always malafidely killing his fellowmen, whereas an animal having brutality does not do so. Therefore, we should either give up rationality or take possession of brutality at least to be the equal of the animal or cultivate and enrich only rationality abandoning brutality to be men in the true sense of the term. Now we sincerely feel that we have utterly failed in our mission and, therefore, we need the help of animals, which may be good and useful to society. But animals have only freedom; they have no knowledge, wisdom and conscience. So we request you to kindly grant the aforesaid four virtues to animals so that they can join hands with us in the matter of changing the disorderly society."

On behalf of all the members present in the meeting, the twelve writers singed the petition. Never before had God received such a petition from humankind. So, He graciously considered the matter and readily granted the virtues only to 50 per cent of the animal population only on experimental basis, in view of food, environment and other problems. This very situation could create curiosity and sensation in the world within a few days. In a few years, these animals got themselves involved in national affairs as other citizens did. They began to make speeches in public meetings. They observed festivals and performed marriage ceremonies. They began to read and write. As they received the great gift from God, they took an active interest in their own development. They earned their living by resorting to different professions as human beings did. In the course of time, they grew in number. Most of them used their knowledge and wisdom in a destructive manner as men did, while the others, in constructive ways. Thereafter, theft, murder and such other heinous events took place in their society. They began to harm even human beings. So in no way they were now better than humankind. Ultimately, they become human-animals because of these four virtues being used in a destructive manner.

The aim and objectives entertained by the aforesaid assembly members were vitiated as human beings or human animals could never be good. Those that transcended their selfish desires alone could be good. This is the reason why there were/are only a few good people in society now. These few people could not do anything good as before.

So now, human-animals and good people assembled in the particular place mentioned above and had a thorough discussion over their vices. At last, they decided to again submit a supplication to God. The twelve human-animals wrote the supplication in the following manner: "Our Beloved God, we thank you that you have granted us certain virtues on account of which we have been able to be equal to human beings in many respects. We could know that you are our God. We understand and feel that we have gone astray and, therefore, we are not worthy to be your children. As per the very purpose of your creation, we should obey you and live in peace with our fellow beings. But as we are living now in a corrupt society of human beings and human animals, we are unable to do so. There is no doubt that we can have a peaceful and holy life provided we come forward to exercise control over our selfish desires, temporal influence and evil forces seeking your grace and power to do so. So, for the time being, the very purpose of your beautiful creation is greatly defeated by the satanic forces and, therefore, higher virtues are necessary to overcome these evils.

"Under the circumstances, as mentioned above, we beseech your Holy Self to graciously grant us super knowledge, super wisdom, super conscience and super freedom, purity of thought and action and great physical, mental and spiritual power and thus help us to build up a superb society where we can have peace and order and where we keep touch with you in our daily life."

God never wants that human beings and human-animals should perish. So He readily granted the aforesaid super virtues to all the human-animals; as a result, they assumed angelic appearance and thenceforth they were called Super Beings. At this juncture we handed over the charge of accomplishing the task of completing this book to the four Super Beings who began to do the needful. However, these four Super Beings were pleased to take three persons from this first panel of seven writers to their group. So again, they were all together seven in number.

CHAPTER II

God, Creation, Man and Religion

Now, human beings were so astonished and jealous of the culture of these Super Beings that they could no longer tolerate their existence. But they could not do anything to them, as they were harmless, powerful and superior to them in all respects and this is the turning point in the history of humankind, which the world had ever seen. The god people welcomed them and whole-heartedly joined them in all their good activities. Rapidly the Super Beings grew in number and began to develop in every sphere of their life. They started constructing and maintaining a society of a high order. They were most practical in their activities. Their first and foremost duty was to assemble at the central place (mentioned earlier) of the world only to praise the Creator. They praised Him in the following manner:

> Praise God, all you nations,
> Thank Him, all you peoples.
> For great is His love towards us,
> And His faithfulness remains forever.

Hear this, all you people,
Listen, all who live in this world,
Both low and high
Rich and poor alike.
Now we will speak words of wisdom,
And do marvellous work for all.
God will strengthen us
To rescue the oppressed
From deceitful and wicked human beings,
And to wipe tears
From the eyes of all.

They chalked out programmes in detail to be executed in their respective lands. After the great assembly they returned home safe and sound and began to do the needful. They never lacked sympathy, imagination, great vision and elasticity in the choice of means. First of all, they wanted us to take up matters like God, creation, religion, food, health, education, economy, sciences and humanities, politics, administration and social transformation and the like in order of acute necessities. Top priority was given to the spiritual development and administration. Of course, they planned to do everything rapidly and simultaneously. At the outset, people could not understand them properly and so they began to make fun of them saying, "A pedal-horse does the same duty even in heaven; what will these so-called Super Beings do?" they questioned. They themselves answered that they would do the same thing in their society what they were doing in the jungle. But the Super Beings outwitted them. They did not like to pay heed to their theories.

Within a few years' time most of them could be highly educated. Voracious readers and eminent writers, great scholars and orators, reputed scientists and statesmen came up to adorn the society. They deeply studied sciences, humanities and all the religious books of the world. They attained super knowledge in all respects. They tried their best to communicate it to all the nations of the world. The gravity, the tone and tune and the undercurrent of the communication or declaration were highly remarkable. They called it 'Cosmic Declaration', which will be spreading like wild fire till the end of anarchy is achieved and all round development of the world is fully experienced. Now the second panel of seven writers began to write down as follows:

God is the creator of the world. He has created animals and all things. He is Almighty. He is not an untouchable force or some unknowable absolute, but a person. He has emotions. He thinks, plans, talks, loves and cares for what He has made. He is holy, kind and merciful and does no wrong. He is an eternal and a jealous God. He is slow in anger. He is a faithful God.

There is only one God. No one has ever seen Him. But He sees everyone. The righteous can very well feel his presence. One cannot hide from Him. He is the master of the universe and the only liberator. He says, 'Apart from me there is no liberator.'

He who has created
The sky and the mountain,
The sea and the fountain,
The flora and fauna
And man and manna is the Liberator
Who alone is capable
Of liberating humankind from
Physical, mental and spiritual bondage.

He loves humanity. He is the best provider. He would wipe every tear. He uses tender and sometimes shocking language. He is not a God of disorder. He disciplines us for our good.

Whatever He does to us, He does only for our good. He cannot be tempted by evil. He loves a cheerful giver. He sends a dramatic call to the righteous to adore and glorify Him and to serve humanity. He gives wide scope to all to be good. He punishes for sin, pride and greed. He says, 'When I act who can reverse it?' He does not sleep. He does not doze. He is totally free from such temptations.

Our worship is due only to God. The heavens declare His glory. Do not blaspheme Him. Each human being is responsible to Him. So we must worship Him and follow His orders. It is unfortunate on the part of the pessimists to deny the existence of God. They lose faith not only in themselves but in Him. They think, 'By hard work we live. Science and technology will help us in every respect. Medicine will cure our diseases. So, one should not believe God.' They fail to understand that strength, knowledge and all such gifts always come ultimately from God, not from hard work or clever dealings alone. G. K. Chesterton says, "Had there been no God the pessimists would not have been there in the world."

You cannot measure the mysteries of God. Sometimes the best man on earth suffers the worst calamities. On many occasions He seems distant and silent. Let us have an illustration to clarify. Your must have seen several maimed persons, bruised and wounded, struggling on the road. Even bad and cruel people of our society wish their recovery. If necessary, they readily come forward to sign petition or do any such things in favour of their recovery. But God who is so kind, loving and capable of healing horrible diseases does not express His holy will for their recovery. Often we get news relating to the death of famine-stricken families. God, being the best provider, is silent over the matter. Do you think that He is unkind, cruel, weak, unjust and wrong? No. Why do you suffer then?

1. Satan causes some suffering. Is Satan more powerful than God? No. Sometimes He allows Satan to create problems for your good. So you suffer.

2. Some people believe that God is weak and powerless to prevent human suffering. Some people assume He runs the world from a distance without personal involvement. But He knows and takes care of each and every individual. Then why do you suffer? It is on account of His fair willingness.

3. God wants to know whether you will continue to trust Him even when everything goes wrong.

4. Suffering does not always come as a result of sin. Sometimes sinless people suffer while the sinful does not. He reserves the rights to exercise His holy will.

5. God is never totally silent to your suffering. He is pleased to relieve you in time.

6. Suffering comes for a higher good. If one trusts God during the time of suffering, one can have victory over Satan and get reward from Him. People suffer in this material world think even today that God lacks concern over their suffering. But righteous people believe that God cares about them.

7. God will reward and punish fairly in a final Judgment after death. Some people do not have a clearly formed belief in and after life. So they expect that God's fairness (His approval or disapproval of people) has to be shown in this life. But many religious books teach that God will reward or punish after death. So the one who believes in Him even during the time of suffering is rewarded liberation.

Some people still hold that God is not kind. So we suffer. Practically He is non-existent, they say. Till the end of their life they will be expressing their grudge and grumbling without being able to free themselves from suffering as they have no control over it. So endure the suffering and get the reward here in this world and in the world to come or condemn God and be condemned to hell. No one under the sky can understand the mind of God or else he will be superior to Him. So it is foolish to criticise or comment over His actions. The Theory of Relativity propounded by Albert Einstein is difficult to understand. So how can you understand the Creator's mind? Therefore, it is not for you to try to reason out the specific cause of a person's suffering. God reserves that knowledge for Himself. So the only way open to you is to pray to Him, to be free from the clutches of such horrible situations and get relief, peace and solace from Him.

Creation of the World

On seeing the sky, the stars, the moon, the sun, the high mountains, the vast sheet of water, the colorful vegetation and the living beings, we question as to who has created all these living beings and things. The answer is that the earth and the other planets have been created from the body of the sun and that human beings and other living creatures are descendants of some of the ancient animals. We cannot correctly say when this world was created. The scientists differ in their opinion. Some of the scientists are of opinion that some portions fell off the body of the sun about four-hundred-and-fifty crore years ago and began to rotate round it with great force. As a result of it the earth, the planets and the sub-planets were created. While some teachers teach this theory in schools and colleges, other teachers teach in a different manner. They say that God has created the world. Now a brilliant student would be in conflict between God's creation and self-perpetuating creation and between religion and science as well.

The pessimists and scientists say that scientific investigation of the world around us has proved that life came into existence not by intelligent creation but by chance and by the process of evolution. They argue, therefore, that there is no creator. Now let us try to refute their argument.

A Simple Approach

1. Something cannot come out of nothing. Drawing says the jellyfish appeared in water. Who created this water and how did the jellyfish come into existence? No satisfactory answer.

2. He says that living beings developed into water-living and land-living creatures. Now there is not a single sign of such phenomena.

3. How is it possible that two different species, say tigers and goats, originated from the fish?

4. Today not a single monkey develops into a man. Some say illogically that there were some particular monkeys in ancient times, which could be human beings.

5. Why do human beings not develop into super beings today? Why and when did this evolution system come to a close?

6. The scientists say that men and other animals appeared on earth millions of years ago. But it is proved from the study of fossils that this creation is not at all as old as they imagine it to be.

A Complex Approach

If there was no Creator, then life must have started spontaneously by chance. For life to have come about, somehow the right chemicals would have to come together in the right quantities. Under the right temperature and pressure and other controlling factors, and all would have had to be maintained for the correct length of time. Furthermore, for life to have begun and been sustained on earth, the chance events would have had to be repeated thousands of times. But how likely is it for even one such event to take place?

Evolutionists admit that the probability of the right atoms and molecules falling into place to form just one simple protein molecule is 1 in 10^{115} or followed by 113 zeroes. That number is larger than the estimated total number of atoms in the universe. Mathematicians dismiss as never taking place anything that has a probability of occurring of less than 1 in 10^{50}. But for more than one simple protein molecule is needed for life. Some 2,000 different proteins are needed just for a cell to maintain its activity and that the chance that all of them will occur at random is 1 in 10^{4000}. "If one is not prejudiced either by social beliefs or by a scientific training into the conviction that life originated spontaneously on earth, this simple calculation wipes the idea entirely out of court," says astronomer Fred Hoyle.

On the other hand, by studying the physical world, from the minute subatomic particles to the vast galaxies, scientists have discovered that all known natural phenomena appear to follow certain basic laws. In other words, they have discovered logic and order in everything that is taking place in the universe, and they have been able to express this logic and order in simple mathematical terms. "Few scientists can fail to be impressed by almost unreasonable simplicity and elegance of these laws, write a professor of physics, Paul Davies, in the magazine *New Scientist*.

A most intriguing fact about these laws, however, is that in them there are certain factors whose values must be fixed precisely for the universe, as we know it, to exist. Among these fundamental constants are the unit of electric charge on the proton, the masses of certain fundamental particles and Newton's universal constant of gravitation, commonly denoted by the letter G. On this, Professor Davies says, "Even minute variations in the values of some of them would drastically alter the appearance of the universe. For example, Freeman Dyson has pointed out that if the force between nucleons (protons and neutrons) were only a few per cent stronger, the universe would be devoid of hydrogen. Stars like the sun, not to mention water, could not exist. Life, at least as we know it, would be impossible. Brandon Carter has shown that very much smaller changes in G would turn all stars into blue giants or red dwarfs, with equally dire consequences for life." Thus, Davies concludes: "In this case it is conceivable that there might be only one possible universe. If that is so, it is a remarkable thought that our own existence as conscious beings is an inescapable consequence of logic."

What can you deduce from all of this? First of all, if laws govern the universe, then there must be an intelligent lawmaker who formulated or established the laws. Furthermore, since the laws governing the operation of the universe appear to be made in anticipation of life and conditions favorable to its sustenance, purpose is clearly involved. Design and purpose— these are not characteristics of blind chance; they are precisely what an intelligent Creator would manifest.

Of course, design and purpose are seen not only in the orderly working of the universe, but also in the way living creatures, simple and complex, carry on their daily activities, as well as in the way they interact with one another and with the environment. For example, almost every part of our human body—the brain, the eye, the ear and the hand—shows design so intricate that modern science cannot fully explain it. Then there are the animal and plant worlds. The annual migration of certain birds over thousands of miles of land and sea, the process of photosynthesis in plants, the development of one fertilized egg into a complex organism with specialised function—just to give a few examples—are all outstanding evidence of intelligent design.

Some argue, however, that increased knowledge of science had provided explanations for many of these feats. True, science has explained, to a certain extent, many things that were once a mystery. But a child's discovery of how a watch works does not prove that the watch was not designed and made by someone. Likewise, our understanding of the marvellous ways in which many of the things in the physical world function does not prove that there is no intelligent designer behind them. On the contrary, the more we know about the world around us the more evidence we have for the existence of an intelligent Creator, God. (From "Mankind's Search For God", pp. 335-40).

One of the eminent scientists of the world, Dr. E.K.Victor Pearce, who has written *Origin and Destiny of Life,* states that the DNA genetic code, which works in the brain, can not be created by humans. Only God can create it.

Now let us go to the Holy Scriptures to know a little more about creation and the creator of the world.

Rig-Veda
"Ognimoule Purohitong Jognosyo debomruhijong hotarong rotnodhatomom"

The substance of this first sloka (verse) of the first Veda, called The Rig-Veda, is as follows: "We are praying to the God who is the Creator of this world and who is worthy of worship in all seasons and times."

Manusmriti
The 'Paramatma' (the Supreme Soul) is described as the creator (the first chapter, the eighth and ninth verses). A gigantic man was created from Brahma of whom Manu was the product. Manu is the ancient man of human beings (First chapter, verses 32 and 33).

The Holy Quran

Allah says, 'Out of the dust we have created you.' (The Teachings of the Holy Quran, p 113, no 5).

The Bible

God Himself has created the sun, the moon, the earth and all the living beings in it (p 1 and 2). God created man in His own image, in the image of God He created him; male and female He created them. (Genesis 1: 27).

Thus the Holy Scriptures also present God as the Creator of the universe. Historians say that on account of the evolution of mammals some kind of apes appeared on earth about five million years ago. In the course of time, these apes changed into more developed beings. These creatures are called early men. They had no wisdom and knowledge. But it is not so. God created men in His own image. So they were developed in all respects. In some areas, they lived in the forest. But never have they been apes or any such other animals. We have already mentioned that man got wisdom, knowledge, conscience and freedom from the beginning. Therefore, he was able to build up a very great civilisation even in the most ancient times. Anthropologically speaking, man is conscious of his own limitations. So he is afraid of nature. Therefore, he tries to take refuge under the supreme. On the other hand, most of the human beings, depending upon their knowledge and freedom, are going against God and their fellowmen. They suppress their conscience. This is the root cause of all troubles on earth and the turning point in the life of every individual.

Was the early man as knowledgeable as the present man? The answer is in the positive. Of course; some of them were innocent and ignorant. Event today, not all human beings are flying or diving. There are still a great many of innocent and ignorant human beings on earth. In the course of time those who lived in the forest and hilly areas due to varied reasons, remained undeveloped; for example, the Bonda Parojas of Malkangir District in Orissa, India. But it is imperative to note that all the civilised and uncivilised human beings owe their origin to the first man who was created by God. It is only the geographical influence that keeps the easterners and the westerns apart; otherwise; the white and the black owe their origin to the man who first appeared on the globe. Once, in a particular place, a curious and a sensational incident took place. A wolf carried away the boy to the jungle. It did not cause any harm to the boy. Rather, it looked after him. He gradually began to develop the quality of animals including walking with hands. He appeared to be almost an animal. It is the environment that influences the colour, face, visage and the like. So we find differences in colour, lifestyles, nature, etc.

In the course of time, human beings grew in number. So they had to move into different parts of the world. Some selected safer areas for fear of their enemies. They were compelled by the circumstances to live in the impassable regions of the world. Thus they were strictly under the influence of Nature. So, even today, we find vast differences between them in their stature, visage, colour, dress, food, etc. Ultimately, they spread all over the world and came to be known as different tribes, clans, races and nations.

It is clear that man has his own limitations. He is weak in every respect. So he depends upon God, while he is in trouble. He says, 'My God, save me from the hands of my enemies. You are my Creator. You are Omnipotent'; this and that especially while you suffer from severe physical pain, and you cry out and call God to relieve you from the pain. To sum up let us say, when the question of subsistence come, you go to God and when the serious question of creation of the universe comes you resort to "Evolution or By chance Theory" as if God could not undertake the work of creation and entrusted it to some other agency. Entertaining this divergent thought is nothing but sailing in two boats. At this juncture, some people may come up and say 'who says that God is not the creator, and the evolution theory is true?' — then it is all right. But you should teach it in schools and colleges. The first chapters of science, geography and history textbooks should be devoted to 'God's creation of the universe. Then in the succeeding chapters, heavenly bodies, the earth crust, the climatic conditions, the flora and the fauna and the achievement of human beings, etc., should find place as they come within the purview of science and humanities. Of course, we find elements of spiritualism in some literature (poems, epics and essays), which has to be enriched and made clearer in the line.

With regard to the teaching of "God's Creation" to the students we may cite the following expert opinion of a particular Education Board.

The Education Board of the Kansas State in the USA seriously felt that the theory of the Origin of the Species by Charles Darwin is baseless and unsubstantial. It, therefore, resolved to stop teaching the theory in schools. On the other hand, the Board decided that the Creation Theory as expounded in the Bible was to be taught to the students, which is being followed in the state since 1999-2000. The members of the Board further stated that even the teacher of Charles Darwin, Adam Shadewig, disapproved the ideas contained in the theory. The theory expresses that millions of years ago, human beings appeared on earth. Some are of opinion that human civilisation is about as old as 6,000 years only. Now many scientists try to prove it basing on the ruins of Noah's ark discovered in the black sea. The ship was wrecked only after two thousand years of God's Creation of the world. The ship reached the mountains of Ararat and rested there as per the order of God. Many scientists and researchers are of opinion that it got wrecked about four thousand years ago.

The governments of different countries of the world are putting stress now on moral and spiritual education with a view to producing good citizens. So unless and until the purpose of God's creation is reflected in textbooks, the very foundation becomes shaky. Some scholars may come up and say that this idea is divergent, paradoxical and challenging to the established thoughts of the scientists. It is clear that even great scientists err. Many such scientists have come to the Creator God at the fag end of their lives. We are expected to use our reason rightly for the attainment of truth and avoidance of error. If people do not accept these scientific and logical ideas and diffuse the glow of this thought we, the super beings, will do it in near future for the welfare of all as it is the call of the hour. Let us be free from confusion, misconception and misleading thoughts. We shall still conduct super researches on it to find out the missing link in near future. *The History of the World* still supplements this chapter.

Religion

It is a vast subject. One finds oneself lost in the vastness of the subject. Religion is a way of life, which leads people to God and enables them to live with Him here in this temporal world and the world to come.

If we go to find out the origin of religion, again we may go astray as some do in case of 'The Creation of the World.' Different people have different ideas about the origin of religion. Some say that human beings were terribly afraid of natural phenomenon. They felt weak to confront with the force of Nature. So they tried to appease it (Nature) by various means in order to protect themselves. This way they began to worship Nature and developed the idea of religion. For centuries, people, more or less, accepted the religious tradition into which they were born and in which they were brought up. Most of them were satisfied with the explanation handed down to them by their forefathers, feeling that their religion was the truth.

In order not to miss the track we are to go through religious books and Holy Scriptures of the world. They lead us along the right way. Some say that the aforesaid books are full of imaginations, stories and myths and such other elements. They are correct to a certain extent. But most of the books and scriptures are full of historical facts and absolute truths. No doubt, human beings like us wrote them. But they were dictated by the power of God to write things down. No one is asked or required to add/delete anything to/from them now. However, you can write commentary, explanations and elucidation, etc, but no addition/deletion to/from the original one.

If we want to grasp the central themes of different religions and find out the Creator God, we are required to read the books concerned slowly and reflectively and then try to gain an excellent overview of some of the favourite chapters. Some of these books say that God created us and revealed Himself to us. He let us know to know Him well. Man began to worship Him in different ways. Some thought of different Gods for different purposes. Some religions do not put stress on God. They attach importance to nature and human conduct.

Some of the records reveal that Mesopotamia was the place where human beings first lived. As the human race dispersed from Mesopotamia, their religious ideas, memories and experiences went with them. In the course of time these were elaborated and changed and become the warp and woof of religion in every part of the world. But people could not altogether leave the original idea, which we find here and there.

Now let us go through certain important contents of some of the religions of the world.

Magic- and Spirit-Centred Religion

In ancient times, people of different parts of the world began to worship the deities. Some citizens like the Athenians even included an unknown deity in their worship. People everywhere have their superstitions and fears. They are afraid of spirits. So in both primitive and modern societies, people have resorted to various means in order to control or appease fearsome spirits and to gain the favour of the benevolent ones. Ultimately, they have made spiritism, black magic and occult their religion. Conjurers, sorcerers and magic—practicing priests were/are held with high esteem although they go, sometimes, to the extent of human sacrifices.

Hinduism

The Hindus believe in gods and goddesses. They claim that Hinduism has 333 million Gods. They worship Brahma, Vishnu, Shiva, Krishna, Durga, Lakshmi, Ganesa, Rama and many other gods and goddesses for their welfare. Although they worship many gods they say that Hinduism is not polytheistic. A. Parthasarathy, an Indian writer, explains: "The Hindus are not polytheistic. Hinduism speaks of one God. The different gods and goddesses are mere representations of the powers and functions of the one supreme God in the manifested world." Hindus say that their 'Dharma' is 'Sanatana Dharma', which means eternal law or order. It is not so easy to understand the Hindu mythology.

In the course of time, the beliefs, myths and legends of India were put into writing. It is called the holy writings of Hinduism. The oldest writings are the Vedas, the Rig-Veda, the Sama-Veda, the Yajur-Veda and the Atharva-Veda. They are a collection of prayers and hymns. They are full of philosophical and spiritual reflections. The Vedas were later supplemented by other writings, including the Brahmanas and the Upanishads. Then two epics 'the Ramayana and the Mahabharata were written. The Bhagavad Gita (celestial song) is a fine instruction of morality. The instructions constitute the supreme way of religion. Non-violence is one of the basic concepts of Hinduism.

Hindus are not supposed to kill or do violence to animals like cows, snakes and monkeys. One of the important aspects of Hinduism is the caste system, which divides society into rigid classes. The untouchables had a very hard existence. Now the caste system has been disappearing from the Indian society since 1948. Mahatma Gandhi's role in the matter of removing the caste system is remarkable.

The Hindus believe that there are four ways of achieving *Moksha* (Liberation):

1. Karma yoga (the way of action)

2. Jnana yoga (the way of knowledge)

3. Bhakti yoga (the way of devotion)

4. Raya yoga (a method of special postures, methods of breathing, and rhythmical repetition of the proper thought formulas). The teaching of Karma (action) plays a very important role in the life of a Hindu. This karma affects a person's destiny. He believes that he cannot fly from the effects of his own prior bad deeds.

In conclusion, we can say that Hinduism has shown that it is a religion of polytheism based on monotheism. It entertains superstitions and mythical gods. It teaches tolerance and encourages kindness towards human beings and animals. On the other hand, some elements of Hindu teachings such as karma and the injustice of caste system and the conflicts in the myths encourage some people to question this issue.

Buddhism

Siddhartha Gautama is the founder of this religion. As a prince he was living a luxurious life. When, for the first time in his life, he saw a sick man, an old man and a dead man, he began to think deeply over the meaning of life. In fact, on seeing the sight, he was mentally agonised. Then he saw a holy man who had renounced the world in pursuit of truth. This holy man looked cheerful, free from worries. This encouraged Gautama to give up his family, his possessions and his kingdom and spend years seeking the truth. He pursued an extreme course of self-denial. Then he preferred to adopt what is called the middle way. He sat in meditation under a tree resisting all temptations. After continuing meditation for about four weeks, he believed that he had transcended all knowledge and understanding and reached enlightenment (spiritual peace). Then he became the Buddha (enlightened). Having attained enlightenment, he set forth to teach his newly found truth.

He taught 'Four Noble Truths':

1. All existence is suffering.
2. Suffering arises from desire or craving.
3. Cessation of desire means the end of suffering.
4. Cessation of desire is achieved by following the Eight-Fold Path, controlling one's conduct, thinking and belief.

The Eight-fold truths are:

- Right views
- Right aspirations
- Right speech
- Right conduct
- Right livelihood
- Right effort
- Right mindfulness
- Right contemplation

Buddhism teaches the way to perfect goodness and wisdom without a personal God. It says that there are no gods who can help man. It is said that on his death bed, the Buddha told his disciples, 'Seek salvation alone in the truth; look not for assistance to anyone besides yourself.' Buddhism ignores the fundamental concept of a Supreme Being by whose will everything exists and operates.

Taoism and Confucianism

Lao-tzu (which means 'old master' or 'old one') is the founder of Taoism. The word 'Tao' means, 'way, road, or path.' Instead of believing in a Creator God who controls the universe; the followers of Taoism believe in providence, a will of heaven. It advocates inaction, quietness, passivity and retuning to nature. Its basic idea is that everything will come out right if people will sit back, do nothing and let nature take its course. The religion says that there is no point in anyone doing anything to interfere with what nature has set in motion. No matter how unbearable a situation is, it will soon become better. Even pleasant situations also fade away in the course of time. Later, the Taoists resorted to magical practices as well. They worship many gods and goddesses. They have temples, monasteries, etc., in the Buddhist fashion. With the passage of time, Taoism slowly changed into a system of idolatry and superstition.

Confucianism

When Taoism degenerated Confucianism gained ground in China. Confucius is the founder of this religion. He put stress on ethics and morals. He felt that ethics could save the troubled world of his day if only the rulers would apply it in their administration. This concept is known as 'li', which means propriety, courtesy and the order of things, ritual, ceremony and reverence. It is a rule of conduct. The Chinese people were greatly influenced by Confucius' thought.

In Confucianism and Taoism, we see how a system based on human wisdom and reasoning falls short in the search for the Creator of God. The Chinese persons know nothing about their personal God. Of course; they are gradually entertaining optimistic thoughts.

Shintoism

It is a Japanese religion. Shintoists worship many gods, as many as eight million gods. The sun-goddess is the central figure of Shinto gods. Harmony with gods, nature and community is an important factor of the religion. Shintoism is a religion of festivals. Shintoists have no specific identification of one God. They also base their belief on mythology. Now some of them are gradually entering the arena of optimism.

Judaism

It is the religion of the Jews. It is full of historical events. In no way it is rooted in mythology; other major religions are indebted to its scriptures. Christianity founded by Jesus has its roots in Hebrew (Jewish) scriptures. Islam also owes much to those scriptures. (Quran, Surah 2:49-57:32:23, 24). The Jewish religion shows the way to the Creator. God chose Abram, the forefather of the Jews, to be his special servant. He blessed him and his family throughout their life. The Jews believe in the Creator. This belief was passed on to Christianity and Islam. God says, 'You shall have no other gods beside Me. (The Bible, Exodus, chapter 20).

The Jews try to find God through scriptures and traditions. The Jewish Bible is called *Torah*. Many Jews do not wait for a personal Messiah (Jesus of Nazareth). Even now many Jews believe that Messiah will come and reign over them prosperous in all respects. They do not believe that Jesus of Nazareth with whom their forefathers discussed about the holy Scriptures two thousand years ago, whom they met many a time and saw his miracles, was Messiah who already came down to the world and then ascended to heaven.

Christianity

The followers of Jesus Christ are called Christians. Jesus is the founder of this religion, and the Bible is the holy book of

Christians. It (The Bible) proves that Jesus was not a myth (Genesis: 22:18:49, 10). Mathew, a former Jewish tax collector, tells us that Jesus was born in Bethlehem of Judea in the days of Herod, the king. In due course, Jesus began to preach the Gospel as the anointed Son of God. By God's power he performed many miracles including rising out of the dead to life.

Jesus knew the great significance of his father's name and gave emphasis to it. He said to the people, 'I have come in the name of my father, but you do not receive me; if someone else arrived in his own name, you would receive that one......' I told you, and yet you do not believe. The works that I am doing in the name of my father, these bear witness about me? (John 5:43; Mark 12:29, 30). Jesus used to tell that he was king and that he had authority over the heaven and the earth. He said, "I am the way, the truth and the life."

God grants salvation through Jesus Christ alone. This is his holy will according to the Bible. The Jews understood Jesus' statements in a temporal sense and at last; crucified him. He was buried, but he resurrected from death on the third day and ascended to heaven. God sacrificed His son's life for the salvation of humanity or else death could not have touched Jesus. God's love of humankind is immeasurable. The Bible is full of events relating to Jesus' wonderful mastery over sin, death, world and the Satan, and above all salvation. Jesus is the Son of God. He says, "My father and I are one." He is God. Now Christians have been divided in many specific denominations. They developed different creeds and dogmas. But what they unanimously believe in is that Jesus Christ is the Saviour/Liberator. They believe in the oneness of God. The Father, the Son and the Holy Ghost form the Trinity. They are three in one and one in three. They are equal in all respects. They maintain a perfect and marvellous unity.

Islam

It is a religion of Muslims. Muhammad founded it. Almost all the historical narratives of the Holy Koran have their Biblical parallels. The principal teaching of Islam is known as 'Shahadah' or confession of faith. Muslims confess that there is no God but Allah; Muhammad is the messenger of Allah. This thought was conveyed 2000 years earlier with the ancient call to Israel: "Listen, O Israel: Jehovah, our God is one Jehova"—The Bible (Deuteronomy 6:4). Jesus repeated this statement about 600 years before Muhammad. Muslims believe that God is supreme.

Five Pillars of Belief of Muslims

1. Belief in one God, Allah (Surah 23 : 116, 117)

2. Belief in angels (Surah 2: 177)

3. Belief in many prophets but one message. Adam was the first prophet. Others have included Abraham, Moses, Jesus and "The Seal of the prophets," Muhammad (Surah 4:136; 33, 40)

4. Belief in Judgment Day (Surah 15:35, 36)

5. Belief in God's omniscience, prior knowledge and determination of all events. Yet, man has freedom of choice in his actions (Surah 9:51). Islamic sects are divided on the issue of free will (Surah 9:51).

The Baha'i Faith

The Baha'i faith is an offshoot of the Babi religion. This group (Babi religion) in Persia (today Iran) broke away from the Shiite branch of Islam in 1844. Baha Ullah formed this religion. Baha'is believe that God has revealed himself to men by means of 'Divine Manifestations', including Abraham, Moses, Krishna, Zoroaster, the Buddha, Jesus, Muhammad, the Bab and Baha Ullah. They believe in the oneness of God. They think that world unity is possible for God. The brotherhood of men and the equality of women are the major features of the Baha'i belief. They believe that one should be obedient to the laws of the county. They are of opinion that the basic principles of all the great religions of the world are in complete harmony and that they differ only in the nonessential aspects of their doctrines (2 Corinthians 6:14; I John 5:19-20).

After going through the contents of different religions of the world, one can easily understand the basic belief of each religion. Now you have to make a comparison of the major religions of the world and investigate God's word in order to find out the Creator. Whether you are Buddhist, Hindu, Muslim, Shinto, Confucian, Taoist, Jewish, Christian, or of any other faith, now is the time to examine your relationship to the living, loving God. Some are prepared to change their faith but they cannot do so due to certain family and social restrictions and problems relating to property, performance of religious rites, caste system, living conditions, threats, separation, marriage and such other things. God, the Creator, enables you to overcome these obstacles.

Religion is personal. Every one of us is responsible for his or her soul. If we go astray, we will alone be condemned to hell, not your family or society. In this context, the life of Valmiki, the great author of the Ramayana, may be viewed. So consult your conscience after being equipped with knowledge. The inherent contradictious, superstition, imagination and mythical thoughts should vanish from the area of the spiritual philosophy of "Makshya" or salvation. They may find place elsewhere. Logic, reason, scriptures pregnant with historical facts, truth and the like should stand.

The Super Beings, the willing ones and we will worship the Creator and Liberator God. We will teach and practice unselfish love. Our religion will be free from politics, conflicts, war and personal violence and the like. We will successfully unite people of every race, language and tribe, as we do not entertain hatred, but love. We serve God not for selfish gain but out of love. We will glorify Him in our activities. We treat that God is love and He is the source of all blessings. We are talking of super beings. Others may entertain any religious philosophy including imaginations and superstitions if it is so convincing and conclusive.

Now, how can you find out the only Creator God? Go through the scriptures of the world thoroughly, try to gain an excellent overview of the subject, search within and find out. God, the Creator, is one hundred per cent capable of meeting all the needs of the entire world population.

Some hold that gods and goddesses of different regions of the world are foreign to one another. They are correct. But God the Creator can never be a foreign God to anyone under the sky. So we cannot say that He belongs to this nation or that nation; this country or that county, and therefore, we have to acknowledge and accept Him as God, the Creator, if not, for this aberrant behavior of ours he shall heavily punish, as he alone is supreme in all respects.

Science and Religion

Science is defined as a systematic enquiry into a particular department of Nature for attainment of truth. Religion is the way of life that leads to God. Science has a paradoxical nature of having a devastating effect of human carnage and an abundant blessing to the rich as well as to the poorest of the poor. Both science and religion aim at investigation of truth. But their approach and manner of enquiry are different. Science attempts to harness nature. It can blow hot and cold at the same time. It is connected with the mind, while religion is associated with the soul. Science deals with matter whereas religion with the soul.

The rapid development of science has changed the very order of the earth. It is tremendously working for the welfare of the people. The great distance that exists between countries and countries has now been shortened by the progress of science. In every sphere, life has become easy. Science never fails to present the other side of the picture too. On account of the development of science man has started thinking that he is the master of the entire situation. He is now thinking of building a nest in a planet. He is rapidly developing pessimistic tendencies. He is nearer science but far away from God. Now some people venture to misinterpret religious faith. Science is rapidly gaining ground in the heart of the people while religion is losing it. Now religion is facing certain problems. The history of religions indicates that no more wars have been fought for any other reasons than for religion. It is because of the misconceptions of the basic principles of religion and fanaticism, etc. Religion can grow luxuriantly without causing harm to one another. It is the man who tries to pollute the religious atmosphere for his own selfish desire. Science fails to humanise people, while religion is capable of presenting full and rich men on the globe.

Science harnesses Nature but man has to harness modern science and technology lest the whole world should be doomed to death within no time. Alfred Nobel invented dynamite to help people working in mines and to construct roads in hilly regions and many other constructive works. But, now, miscreants are using it to blow up their fellowmen and their property. Science can still do wonders if it is tempered with religion. Science without religion is both charmless and lifeless. Science cannot understand God and religion, heaven and hell. They are not imaginary words. They do exist. There are no greater things as "Makshya" (liberation). Religion leads us to liberation. Some of the greatest scientists are spiritual men. Einstein always believed, that "a great scientific discovery is a matter of religious insight." Dr. C. V. Raman has remarked, "My great discoveries have not come to me in my laboratories but during the time I was away from them, basking in the sunshine of a sea-beach." Almost all scientists come to religion at the fag end of their life. Science and religion should not be contradictory to each other.

Every responsible citizen should try to build up a 'world community'. Man should use science to celebrate victory over war and thus establish peace in society. Science cannot come out of nothing. It depends on objects to flourish, and God creates the natural objects and the like. If science is to flourish and help humankind to soar high like an eagle, it has to depend on religion and spiritual transformation. Any science, which is not tempered with religion, is not science at all. This sort of science would be nothing short of a gigantic giant that would destroy the magnificent creation.

CHAPTER III

Hades, Paradise, Heaven and Hell

A vast majority of the people believe that heaven and hell are real. Some people are of opinion that they are only imaginary objects. Life should be fully enjoyed here in this world itself. Death is the end of everything. Again we have to depend on the Scriptures of different religions to know more about them. Before going into religious dogmas, let us start from what some of the great thinkers of the world have said about heaven and hell.

Senaka (BC 02-65)
Senaka, a Roman philosopher, expounds his thoughts through these interrogative sentences: Have we ever thought about the aim of our life and idealism? What is the shape and image of God? After our death, where will our soul go? He puts stress on the necessity of the right conduct in life. This is a sort of stoicism.

Isaac Bashevis Singer
He says, let our children grow while knowing the difference between God and Satan, the distant between holiness and sinfulness and the gap between heaven and hell.

Now let us come to the details basing on some of the scriptures of different religions. Scriptures declare, "Without religion a house is a burial ground though it is a palace."

Hinduism

Are heaven and hell real? Such doubts haunt the minds of most seekers. Hinduism affirms that they are real as long as the *jiva* has not realised its self-identical, absolute nature.

That we have a moral sense, however faint, should point to the fact that, after all, certain action of ours is 'moral' as yet others 'immoral'. Says Socrates, "The highest science is that which teaches us the distinction between good and bad." This is the rationale of the Law of Karma, which is inexorable operative for all who are not pure enough to be 'Fine Being'.

Purana, Gita, etc., speak of hell in unmistakable terms. Demoniacal people are thrown into the 'wombs of demons' (Gita XVI-19). Lust, anger and avarice are the ways to hell. The one who gives them up and minds the Supreme will get liberation (Gita XVI-22). Similarly heaven is assured, albeit temporarily, for good doers (Gita VI-40). They are assured of excellent birth, etc (Gita VI-41 & 42).

The Law of Karma, as Mahatma Gandhi puts it, is inexorable and impossible of evasion. However, the Law of Karma can be completely rendered negative only through pure knowledge, Brahma Gnana, through Brahma Vidya, which is all about the real identity of people. Then 'merit', 'demerit', 'sin', 'virtue' and such value- based epithets shall cause to have any significance. All relativities and dualisms are transcended as one attains the Absolute (Gita II-72).

Islam

In Koran, mention has been made more than one hundred times about heaven and hell. Those who do good will attain heaven, while bad people will be condemned to hell (Koran-Surah Bakra, No. 81-83).

Christianity

The Bible speaks of four phenomena instead of two. They are the Hades, the Paradise, the Heaven and the Hell.

In English, 'Hades' is called 'Grave', in Hebrew, 'Sheol' and in Greek, 'Hades'. This is a dark and shadowy place. The Israelites were of the opinion that God has no relation with this place. But He has (Revelation 1:18, and Psalm 88:12). After death the soul goes to this place. This Hades is divided into two regions: bad region and good region. Sinners go to the bad region to dwell there (Ezekiel 32-21 and Luke 16:23). The righteous go to the good region. (Refer the life of Lazarus; Luke 16:19-31). After a temporary sojourn in this good place, the righteous would go to Paradise. It is comparatively a better place.

In English, 'Paradise' is called 'Paradise' and in Greek, "Paradeisos". The word *Paradise* comes from the Iranian language—*Pairideza*. It means a wall-surrounded orchard. It is a beautiful place with trees, flowers, fruits, streams and different kinds of birds and animals (Genesis Chapters 1-3). Here miseries and sorrows have no place (Revelation 21: 4). This is a beautiful Garden of Heaven. Even a criminal, who is penitent is very well entitled by Jesus Christ to attain a place in Paradise (Luke 23: 42-43). Then he, the criminal said, "Jesus, remember me when you come into your Kingdom". Jesus answered him, "I tell you the truth, today you will be with me in Paradise".

In Hebrew, 'Heaven' is called 'Samayim' and in Greek, 'Ouranos'. It is a place of eternal bliss. It is an abode of God (Deuteronomy 26:15). God is the Creator of this place. There are many heavens without differences among them. They are just like different suites of a big building. The angels and the other people who are in-charge of different works live in different apartments. The same supreme happiness governs in every room. Genesis 1:1 says, "In the beginning God created the heavens and the earth. 1 Kings 8:27 says, "But will God really dwell on earth?" The heavens, the highest heavens cannot contain you. This plurality is found in Hebrews 4:14 as well: "I know a man in Christ who fourteen years ago was caught up to the third heaven." Just as some righteous men were taken to Paradise so also Elijah and Enoch are the only persons who got access to heaven directly without physical death. As Elijah and Elisha were walking along and talking together; suddenly a chariot of fire and horses of fire appeared and Elijah went up to heaven in a whirlwind (2 Kings 2:11). Why at all is one not allowed to enter directly to heaven? It is so because one's consciousness of God will be limited even here in Paradise since one's body will still be in the good part of the Hades until the day of the great judgment.

"About eight days after Jesus said this; he took Peter, John and James with him and went up to a mountain to pray. As he was praying, his face changed, and his clothes became as bright as a flash of lightning. Two men, Moses and Elijah, appeared in glorious splendour, talking with Jesus. They spoke about his departure, which he was about to bring to fulfillment at Jerusalem. Peter and his companions were very sleepy, but when they became fully awake, they saw his glory and the two men standing with him. As the men were leaving Jesus, Peter said to him, "Master, it is good for us to be here. Let us put up three shelters – one for you, one for Moses and one for Elijah." (He did not know what he was saying).

While he was speaking, a cloud appeared and enveloped them, and they were afraid as they entered the cloud. A voice came from the cloud saying, "This is my son, whom I have chosen: listen to him. When the voice had spoken, they found that Jesus was alone. The disciples kept this to themselves, and told no one at that time what they had seen." (Luke 9: 28-36).

Here it is clear that Moses had come down from the Paradise because he was not taken to heaven as per the Bible, whereas Elijah was taken up to the heaven as quoted above. Moses' consciousness of God is limited in Paradise. So he has to stay there in the Paradise till the judgment day. But righteous as he is, he, too, is entitled to move with the heaven-dwellers as per the holy will of God.

Hell is a horrible place of eternal sorrows, miseries and torment. It is exclusively meant for the sinners. Luke 16: 23 says that the time came when the beggar died and the angels carried him to Abraham's side. The rich man also died and was buried. In hell, where he was in torment, he looked up and saw Abraham far away with Lazarus (the beggar) by his side. So he (the rich man) called to him, "Father Abraham, have pity on me and send Lazarus to dip the tip of his finger in water and cool my tongue, because I am in agony in this fire."

"But Abraham replied, 'Son, remember that in your lifetime you received your good things, while Lazarus received bad things, but now he is comforted here and you are in agony. And besides all this, between us and you a great chasm has been fixed, so that those who wait to go from here to you cannot, not can anyone over from there to us.' He answered, 'Then I beg you, Father, send Lazarus to my father's house, for I have five brothers. Let him warn them, so that they will not also come to this place of torment.' Abraham replied, 'They have Moses and the Prophets; let them listen to them.' 'No, Father Abraham', he said, 'but if someone from the dead goes to them, they will repent.' He said to him, 'If they do not listen to Moses and the Prophets, they will not be convinced even if someone rises from the dead."

Let us analyse this text.

- Abraham was also in Paradise and Lazarus, the beggar, was taken to this place by the angels because he lived a righteous life although his worldly life was very miserable; whereas the rich man enjoyed his life fully forgetting God. So he was condemned to hell.

- The gap between heaven and hell cannot be bridged.

- The rich man is struggling to inform his family about the horrible place in hell.

- Some people are never prepared to listen to the word of God during their lifetime even if one rises from the dead and goes to them to inform the horrible situation of hell and show the way to escape from its clutches.

Did Jesus not rise from the dead and preach about heaven, hell and salvation?

Let us know more about hell. Revelation 21:8 says, "But the cowardly, the unbelieving, the vile, the murderers, the sexually immoral, those who practice magic arts, the idolaters and all liars – their place will be in the fire lake of burning sulfur."

One can still have a vivid and graphic picture of hell in Mathew 5:21-30 and 13:36-43 and in many other books of the Bible.

Matters relating to hell and heaven may be summarised as follows:

- Hell is really the most terrible place.

- Men are not very much serious and conscious about it.

- It has the eternity quality. On earth any trouble may subside in the course of time by God's holy will. All troubles have their own end on the advent of death. Then begins the endless torture for sinners in hell.

- Since God is the just judge, no influence, riches, gifts, bribes, lies, cunningness, knowledge, wisdom, laws and all such things will be of any use before the Omniscient God.

- Repentance for sin, right conduct, faith and above all, the Grace of God alone can save sinners (This is mostly the dogma of Christianity).

- Supreme happiness governs in heaven for eternity. So beware of hell, which is the most horrible place, and follow the ways of the Supreme for heaven!

CHAPTER IV

History of the World

We will take a look at the broad features of man's creation, man's original place and civilisation.

Defining History

J. E. Swain defines history as follows: It attempts to evaluate all the developments in science, in art, in literature, in philosophy, in architecture, in sociology, in politics, in war, in religion and in law. It sketches as complex a picture as possible of everything that has influenced man directly or indirectly.

History has not always been so broadly interpreted. For a long time, historians were concerned primarily with politics. Freeman, an eminent English historian of the 19th century, defined history as 'past politics.' Herodotus, the first great historian, neglected social and economic forces and over-emphasised the personal element. Today, students of history disagree as to which of the various phases is the most important. The economic determinists claim that 'the fundamental condition of all life is economic, while the hero worshippers and others think that the individual is all-important. These are extreme points of view: the first is fatalistic, neglects ethical forces and minimises the importance of great men; the second fails to recognise the fact that great men do not produce the age but are manifestations of it. The correct interpretation of history proceeds from a combination of the two in a modified form. History has been distorted for selfish purposes. The historian is likely to exaggerate the history of his own country.

Some writers consider "History is the record of achievement of man." Others define it in the following manner: "History is the record of various kinds of past activities of humankind in the family, society and in the country in different phases of time."

The Beginning

Every Christian is familiar with the biblical story of the creation of the earth. This has already been dealt with in the foregoing chapters.

Aristotle, Ptolemy, Copernicus, Kepler, Newton and Einstein have explained the origin of the universe. But it remains incomplete. There should not be a conflict between science and religion. Many of the early accounts of creation try to prove that man took place in eons of time. But he was made of clay through the handiwork of God. The Bible says that man was shaped from common clay and that God breathed into his nostrils the breath of life.

According to an old Babylonian legend, God Bel cut off his own head and the other gods took his blood, mixed it with clay and produced man – a creature partly divine because he possessed the blood of god. Some Australian primitive black men believe that the creator molded human forms from a common substance and breathed into them the breath of life. In Greek mythology, Prometheus is recognised as the creator of man as well as of other animals. One of the Upanishads describes a procreator; "Verily, he had no delight; one alone had no delight; he desired a second. He was, indeed, as large as a woman and a man closely embraced. He caused that self to fall into two pieces; therefore, arose a husband and a wife." Similar stories can be found among primitive people in New Zealand, Tahiti, Burma and Siberia.

The Fertile Crescent

It is a crescent-like semi-circle reaching from Sinai to the Tigris-Euphrates river basin. This Fertile Crescent is the only land suitable for agriculture in the whole of south western Asia. It is called Mesopotamia.

The western part of the Fertile Crescent is a vast plain with abundant facilities for agriculture. The grasslands bordering the desert furnished grazing for flocks and the sea invited tradesmen to seek profits through trading with other peoples. So a mixture of cultures developed in this area.

The Hittites, the Aramaneans, the Hebrews (Israelites) and the Phoenicians were the most important peoples who inhabited the western part of the Fertile Crescent in early times. The Hebrew was Semitic. They had inter-marriage with the other groups. The Phoenicians were closely related to the Hebrews and the Armenians, but they confined their settlements to the Syrian coast on the northeast corner of the Mediterranean Sea.

The Hebrews established their kingdom in Palestine. The northern part, Israel, had some fertile valleys and the people were comparatively prosperous. In the southern part, Judah, which had insufficient rainfall, the soil was barren and rocky.

The Israelites were worldly and materialistic in their philosophy and religion. They lived a life of luxury and worshipped the 'golden calf'. God ruled over all and was the source of political as well as religious authority.

Their wonderings and sufferings enabled the Hebrews to develop a religion upon which rests the foundation of Christianity.

Jehovah is the God of the Hebrews. He was the only God. He gave his chosen people the Ten Commandments to conduct their lives properly.

Work of the Prophets

Amos, Isaiah, Jeremiah and Ezekiel—all tried to reveal the Creator and Liberator God.

Isaiah prophesied: "Behold, a virgin shall conceive and bear a son and shall call his name Immanuel."

The Hebrews believed Jehovah as the universal God. They anticipated Messiah (Jesus Christ) to come to the world.

Literature and Learning

The Old Testament—the greater part of Hebrew literature–is concerned with religion, and the works it includes are generally regarded as religious documents. Aside from its spiritual value, however, the Old Testament is one of the greatest and most beautiful pieces of literature produced by any people of any time. As history, it ranks with the works of Herodotus and Gibbon and as poetry, it ranks with the works of Shakespeare and Goethe. The Book of Exodus is an autobiography of Moses, according to tradition. The book of Joshua is an epic depicting the exploits of a hero and the history of a people. The book of Judges contains the dramatic story of Samson. Women, their position and character, are pictured with tender pathos in the book of Ruth. The book of Job is a powerful dramatic narrative with man, Satan and God as the chief characters. The book of Psalm, some of which every Christian knows, is poetry rarely excelled. Psalm 13, for example, is a superb didactic poem.

To the Chief Musician. A Psalm of David.

How long wilt thou forget me, O Lord? Forever? How long wilt thou hide thy face from me?

How long shall I take counsel in my soul, having sorrow in my heart daily? How long shall mine enemy be exalted over me?

Consider and hear me, O Lord my God; lighten mine eyes, lest I sleep the sleep of death.

Lest my enemy say; I have prevailed against him, and those that trouble me rejoice when I am moved.

But I have trusted in thy mercy, my heart shall rejoice in thy salvation.

I will sing unto the Lord, because he hath dealt beautifully with me.

The Book of Proverbs contains many gems of thought.

Happy is the man that findeth wisdom,

And the man that getteth understanding.

For the gaining of it is better than gaining of silver,

And the profit thereof greater than fine gold.

The New Testament

Although the New Testament belongs to a latter period, essentially it, too, is a Hebrew contribution. It is a portrayal of the life and teachings of the great Apostles. Paul is responsible for and is the chief figure in much of the New Testament literature.

The Apocalypse–the Revelation of St John, the Divine, is mystical work in which there is a promise of the Holy City, to succeed this sinful world. (This "History of the world" is taken from "A History of World Civilization" by J. E. Swain).

J. E. Swain has given many accounts of man's origin. He wants to present his documentary proof pertaining to the creation of man with a very sincere, imperative and effective tone narrating that man (the first man) is the handiwork of God. We are to remember that he writes the oldest history and relies on the Scriptures, mostly the Bible (The Old and the New Testaments). The Scriptures are the legs of history without which it cannot stand. History should begin from the origin of the universe and man. It mostly owes its origin to the Scriptures. The very first chapter of the Bible is very clear in the matter of creation of the world and of man. That God created man is beyond doubt and that this matter as well as the Darwinian Theory has been sufficiently dealt with in the foregoing chapters.

Mesopotamia is the Fertile Crescent as mentioned by the historian Swain. It is now known as Iraq. In Mesopotamia was Eden (God's garden) where the first couple was directed to live in. Four rivers including Euphrates (mentioned by swain) watered the garden. In the course of time, Adam and Eve, the first couple, produced children and then the population grew in number at different stages of human history (Genesis chapter 5, from Shem to Abram; Genesis chapters 11&12). After few centuries Abraham, the ancient father of all, came to the picture. God (Jehovah) called him to do His job. The Hebrews are the Jews. Later they were called the Israelites, the chosen people of God. Some people argue that Adam was not the first man. They say 'Adam' means 'man'. It is true. Since great many men were there at that time—they argue—Adam should have been named. Can anyone say the name of the second man who was created by God? Since there was only one man, 'Adam', it was not at all necessary to name him. He was very well known and was called 'Adam' (man) by God himself, who created him. There was no one else to go by this name. Alone as he was, he would have gone by any name. Then his wife was created by God. Her name was Eve (life and not woman). She could have very well gone by the name 'woman'. But according to the holy will of God she was named 'Eve' (life and not woman).

Now, what about their sons and others? Were they 'man' 'and' 'woman'? No. Names were given by their parents (Adam and Eve) right from the first born to the last of the descendants (Genesis, chapters 4 & 5). So, such argument can be dismissed.

They are all the descendants of Abraham. Isaac was the son of Abraham, and Jacob, the son of Isaac. Jacob had 12 sons. 'They are Rueben, Simeon, Judah, Issachar, Zebulun, Ephraim, Benjamin, Joseph (Manasseh), Dan, Asher, Naphtali and Gad. The descendant of these Israelites spread over Canaan, the Promised Land and then, all over the world. Since there was great famine in Canaan (the native and promised land of the Israelites), the sons of Jacob moved to ancient Egypt and lived there for about 500 years. During this period they were tortured by the pharaohs, the great rulers. On seeing their miserable condition, God (Jehovah) liberated them from the bondage of the aforesaid rulers under the leadership of Moses who led them to return to Canaan (later called Palestine), where they peacefully lived defeating the inhabitants of the country in battles. The details of their return journey are clearly mentioned in the Bible (Number, chapter 33.)

First of all, the people lived a nomadic life. Some of them resorted to agriculture. It is the agriculture that brought settled life in the history of humankind. According to the scriptures they were civilised people. The Scriptures are silent about the Paleolithic age. God-made man can never be uncivilised. (Genesis 4: 21-22). "His brother's name was Jubal; he was the father of all who played the harp and flute. Zillah also had a son, Tubal-cain, who forged all kinds of tools out of bronze and iron." This is the beginning. One may question as to why then we find even in the 21st century a charcoal seller who is as primitive as an animal. This has already been dealt with. The literature and learning highlighted by Swain based on documents proves the enlightenment of the people.

Migration is an inherent quality of men. They grew in number, migrated to different parts of the world according to their suitability. They underwent geographical influences, which led them to assume different colours, resort to different food habits and, as they were mental beings, they began to think of higher life and living. They observed the natural phenomena like the sun, the moon, the great mountains, the clouds and the vast sheets of waters, etc., and began to think of different makers. The advanced people concluded that different gods and goddesses must have made different objects of the great Nature. They began to worship them. Philosophical thoughts still developed and crept into society as a result of which emerged different religions and cultures in different parts of the world.

Dr. Joab Lohora writes in his book, *Bible Birodhavasha Baikalpika* (Oriya p 216), which was published in October 2000, that according to the research works of Dr. Manasseh there is a saying in India that the Brahmins are the descendants of Abraham. Keturah, the concubine of Abraham (Genesis 25.1), was Hittitite. The Hittitites were Indian-Aryans. Their sons made an exodus from Abraham to the East (Genesis 25:6). India is in the East of Arabia.

Thus people were scattered the world over and entertained different religions and cultures.

Most people might not know that the history of the world owes its origin mostly to the Bible. They think that it is only a scripture. The names of persons and places mentioned in world history are not imaginary persons, figures and places. Some of the cities and places are still in existence even today. So legends and imaginations have no place in this context.

CHAPTER V

Language and Literature

Literature

People say that literature is the reflection of life and society. Some, ironically, say that it is a projection of one's personality. The literature and language of human beings are so rich, the standard of their writing is so high, the style is so jargonistic and the process of communications is so complicated that a great many of common readers find themselves lost in the vastness of such technical matters and literary technology. Some of the writers are now interested in the use of computers, which can produce high-sounding and unintelligible words and phrases. Sometimes writers cannot understand their own works, what to speak of readers' comprehension. Some poems, novels and essays are specially made complicated as if they were meant only for poets and writers and not for the reading public. Why do such things happen? In some cases, projection of ability and reputation in the field of literature encourages them to do so. Perhaps, such bombastic and high-sounding language is necessary in some spheres but not in the common area. This situation attracts one and all. Some writers possess superb quality of producing good literature in all respects.

Definitions vary from scholars to scholars. But they try to touch the very connotation of the term.

Since we would like to communicate our ideas to the peoples of all nations, high and low, very clearly, we would prefer to be simple but forceful and clear in our expressions. Moreover, it is not necessary now for us nor for the people to maintain such a high standard of literature while our soul aim is to remove bad elements from the world community. Later, we shall pay attention to a more chaste, elegant and highly polished language.

Subject Matter of Literature

Instead of floating in the realm of imagination, the writer may collect materials from the reality of life. Every day they come across many incidents taking place in the world. Newspapers are full of incidents pertaining to ill treatment of parents by their children and misbehavior of children towards their parents, dowry tortures, kidnapping, rape, murder, theft, war pestilence, famine, poverty, terrorism, people of different attitudes and philosophy of life, sociology, science, technology and the like. One can very well collect rare gems from these mines. The real names of good and bad persons appear in newspapers. One can change their names and have a plot of one's own giving flesh and blood to it. Try to touch every aspect of human life.

Since books are the keys to the door of knowledge and writers are the most powerful and honest constructors of society, they (writers) should aim at nothing but producing moral stalwarts and spiritual giants in society. Now we find many spiritual dwarfs, moral bankrupts and antisocial elements in society. Of course, it is not so on account of sub-standard literature only, but also for the heinous activities of some other agencies, which we will discuss later. Of course, the morale generated by most of the authors is praiseworthy. Favoritism and slavish mentality should not find place in literature. Truth and life have their supreme value.

From time immemorial the subject of love has dominated the field of world literature. A number of writers are especially interested in erotica. Most of the works of Kalidasa and Upendra Bhanja (Indian writers) come, to some extent, under this category. If you study "As You Like It" by Shakespeare, you can conclude that among all human passions it is love that alone finds entrance in the Forest of Arden. Many writers and readers are of the opinion that literature bereft of love is dead and a colourful description of the element of love lends a special charm to the scene. It is most welcome. But what kind of love is it? It is imperative to know the answer. H. G. Bridges says that "love is a fire in whose devouring flames all earthly ills are consumed." Most welcome is this love. Mainly, there are four kinds of love. Let us use some Greek words to explain it.

- *Eros*: It means the love of a man for a maid and vice-versa; it is the love that has passion in it.

- *Philia*: It is the warm love that you feel for your nearest and dearest; it is a thing of the heart.

- *Storge*: It means affection that specially exists in the hearts of parents and their children.

- *Agape*: It means loving your fellowmen although they might harm you in many ways; it is a feeling of the mind as much as of the heart; it concerns the will as much as the emotions; it describes the deliberate efforts that one can make only with the help of God; and it connotes God's love for His children and vice versa.

Now, which love is mostly reflected in our literature? We think it is *eros*. An *eros*-dominated literature creates an *eros*-dominated society. And, practically, we are having this situation in certain spheres. So let us try our best to produce *philia, stroge* and *agape* in our literature and save society from utter destruction.

Qualities of Good Literature

- Literature should aim at constructing society; it should have a reformative character; it should not lack vision and insight.

- It should be life-touching; originality has its special value.

- It should reflect the life of society.

- It should aim at producing good citizens; it should teach no war but peace.

- It should be able to present rich and full human begins on the globe, giving them an idea of liberation from physical, mental and spiritual bondage.

- It should aim at improving one's international outlook and cosmic view.

- It should not be bereft of innocent or pure pleasure; it should make readers inquisitive to be able to discover the value of literature and unfold their latent talents.

- It should have literary value; the language should be lucid, elastic and enriched by words and phrases borrowed from many languages.

- It should reflect the aforesaid four kinds of love focusing on the last category; elevated sentiments should dominate the erotic sentiment.

- Spiritualism and ethics are the pivot around which literature should revolve.

Growth, Development and Extinction of Languages

Some say that there are now about seven thousand living languages in the world and several thousand (almost the same number) languages are dead. Some scholars are of the opinion that the Semitic language is the oldest one in the world. It consisted of many languages.

Let us take a look at the reasons of the extinction of languages. One of the major reasons is lack of interest and feeling of inferiority complex in the matter of speaking certain languages. We visited certain remote villages in Koraput district, Orissa, and found that the old people had been using their original tongue whereas the younger generation of the same villages had not been doing so, especially in urban areas. That was because of the development of some sort of complex and a peculiar attitude towards their own tongue. They were shy of speaking 'Mafasalia' or 'Desiya' (a mixture of Oriya and a sort of Oriya that appears to be akin to the common Oriya language.) These people used to be criticised by some people for speaking this language. If such a partly understandable language is misspelt, mispronounced or wrongly used, the speakers are criticised. So, instead of extending its boundary, it (the language) limits itself to the original area or gradually loses certain portions. We encouraged them to speak the language publicly and make it a living one. Of course this ill feeling is gradually vanishing from such areas due to varied reasons, including attempts by the benevolent government, writers, social workers and the like to preserve the language and culture and, above all, for their present self-consciousness.

Once in a particular law court in the Koraput District, Orissa, a curious incident took place. In short, the following is the case. A villager, probably from Naugaon village, had gone to a nearby village to thrash mustard seeds. On his return home during lunch-hour, he had a quarrel with another man of the same village. This hungry and tired thrasher grew angry and charged the other on the head with big sticks used for thrashing corns. Unfortunately, it resulted in the death of the man.

Now the case came up to the law court for trial. The advocate for the deceased had no knowledge of the *Desia* language (This peculiar mixture, as a whole, appears to be neither Oriya nor broken Oriya nor non-Oriya like the tribal languages). The advocate asked the witnesses of Nuagaon (place of incident) as to why at all the deceased had been to the particular village. They answered *sorshu pity jayirela*. It means that he had gone to the village for the thrashing of mustard seeds. The advocate submitted to the court misinterpreting that he had gone to a village called 'sorshupity'. Then the advocate put the second question as to who else had seen the incident. The witnesses answered that 'gulagnar lok deklaie.' It means that people of the whole village saw the incident. The advocate again stated wrongly before the Hon'ble court that the people of the village, 'Gulagaon' saw the incident. After hearing the case, the Hon'ble court correctly observed that the witnesses of Nuagaon and not of Gulagaon or any other village should, at this stage, come to give evidence. The Honourable Court ordered for retrial with proper care and correct information.

Let us reveal the meaning of *Sorshu piti jairela* (he had gone for thrashing of mustard seeds), *Sorshu-sorisho* in Oriya and mustard seeds in English; *piti-pitiba* in Oriya and beating (thrashing). If English, *jai-jai* in Oriya and going in English; *rela-rohila* or *thila* in Oriya and was in English. So *jairela* means *jaithila* in Oriya and 'had gone' in English. You can very well mark that these *Desia* words are akin to standard Oriya.

Such serious problems, as illustrated above, arise out of ignorance of certain languages. Although we are not acquainted with some of such languages, we try to meddle with them for our selfish/unselfish ends and thus enter into complexity and confusion. This may also be the reason why some people, who do not know such languages, are not interested in them (languages). People speaking these languages of their own also shrink into the corner of their society without plucking up a sort of courage to speak them publicly. As a result, the spread and development of them (language) are at stake.

Perhaps, seriously viewing such horrible situations, some of the law courts have now appointed interpreters, especially to interpret some tribal languages, which are foreign to many of us. A few years ago, we met a gentleman who was on the way to the court. On being asked he let us know that he was one of the interpreters. Misinterpretations of facts due to language-complexity enable the culprit to leave the court singing and dancing while the blood-relatives of the deceased (or the imprisoned) return mourning.

In many parts of the world, people belonging to different areas, races, cultures, etc., use different languages as their mother tongues. Most of them do not understand the regional/ national language. They do not understand even a bit of the other languages except their mother language. Very recently, we found some such people, perhaps coming from a remote corner of Andhra Pradesh to a particular Oriya-speaking area. They could not understand even a bit of Oriya or Hindi or English (even only a few words). They are fluent in their mother tongue, Telugu. This is only an example.

Here is a funny story related to the language problem. The Bonda Parojas, who are comparatively still primitive, live in the highlands of the Malkangiri District, Orissa, India. About five years ago, one of the Bonda honey-sellers had come over to Jeypore (Orissa) to sell honey. He used a particular measurer for honey worth Rs. 5 only. He could neither know the use of fraction selling nor was able to calculate the price. What he did was collection of only five-rupee notes from the purchasers. He knows not any other language except his mother tongue, 'Bonda language'.

Thus the language trades seriously suffer for want of smooth management of exports and imports systems.

Language Problems

- If people, including students, take more interest in the language other than their mother tongue, it (mother-tongue) would begin to gradually decay. We find several articles frequently appearing in newspapers referring to this problem, especially, in the state of Orissa. Sometimes parents themselves encourage their children to learn the second or the third language more and more. They (parents) do not put much stress on their mother tongue. In this context, you find a sort of criticism relating to English language schools.

- Calamities such as earthquakes, volcanic eruptions, terrible diseases and wars— in such pitiable circumstances life and language go together.

- Each and every language has idiomatic expressions, sayings, parlance, proverbs, meaningful and ethical/moral tenets, etc. A very few people, especially the old ones, are capable of using these expressions in a fitting manner. The younger generation takes interest neither to know nor to use them in their day-to-day conversations.

- If the government, writers and others do not encourage the growth, development and enrichment of a particular language, it becomes extinct.

- Sometimes victorious countries try their best to introduce their own languages as national languages in the defeated countries. So, the foreign language begins to flourish and the native language suffers due to lack of patronage. Due to such varied reasons many languages are gradually vanishing from society. Soon the beautiful universe is going to lose its charm following the extinction of languages. The language problem is compared to environmental crisis. Just as a ship does not sink within a few hours, so also the language of a particular tribe or people does not become extinct within a month or two. The scope is wide; the time at our disposal is not short, though not long. So let us do the needful.

- If leadership is vested in the hands of administrators whose mother tongues are not the language of a particular state or a country, they may not take interest in the growth and development of the language in question. Sometimes, a sort of politics may creep into the matter to worsen the condition of the language.

Solutions to Language Problems

- One should be conscious of making one's own language, whether polished, colloquial, spoken or tribal, lively, lovely and alive by various means.

- The inferiority complex in the matter of using one's own language should go.

- Natural calamities may not altogether take away any language. Let us collect the fragments of the dying language and assemble it.

- Collect the rare gems of idiomatic expressions, etc., from the good old persons and keep them on record.

- Earnestly request and encourage writers and other wise men to produce good literature.

- Different students/people have different tastes, interest and ability for the learning of a particular language. Allow them to freely do so without causing harm to their normal routine.

- Nowadays the voice of colonialism is feeble. So, there is virtually no such problem of developing a particular language in a particular state or country.

- A blend of different languages/literatures and cultures may solve the problems.

- Different languages for the development of a state or a country should be taught at schools and colleges, viz. regional, national and international. Of course, it is not new information, as many countries have already adopted this system. But there should be no deviation from following the procedure for the three-language formula.

- Special treatment should be given to the people to learn the second language (first being the mother-tongue).

In 1999, while addressing some of the educated youths of the undivided Koraput District in Koraput itself, we urged them to learn at least six languages, viz. their original mother tongue (*Desia*, akin to Oriya), the other Desia language (there are two main Desia language in the district, one spoken in the highland and the other in the plain areas of the same district, besides many tribal languages), Telugu (the language of the immediate neighboring state called Andhra Pradesh, Oriya (state language of Orissa), Hindi (national) and English (international). Then, if their capacity and time permit them, they may still learn as many developed languages as they can, we added. They may not be proficient in three languages; it may be only a question of managing the situation. But they must know well the other three languages, viz. their original mother tongue, Oriya and Hindi.

Also, statesman-spirit and administrative will and zeal should be established in the area of improvement of the language.

Conclusion

Since language and literature are a unifying factor, since they improve the international outlook and cosmic view, since they sincerely attempts to liberate humankind from various bondages and since they are capable of constructing society in all respects, we should resourcefully see that they thrive and grow luxuriantly.

We know that language, literature, art, culture and the like do not directly flourish on their own. So, the public and the government have to be involved in the matter of sowing seeds, germination, growth and development of the language. Of course, the role of the writers, authors, artists and the like is very special and superbly remarkable. They can produce wildfire as well as cool, sparkling, crystal waters through literature and art, keeping in view the need and condition of society. They can make the people—the audience and the readers—laugh, weep and think. They sincerely try to create high tides, not to cause floods of destruction but to begin a new voyage to move on to 'fortune'.

Thus the great brain that was once capable of eradicating the evils of society, the reformative tone and the commanding voice that could remove superstitions and undesirable practices of society and establish truth; the great talent that was able to give insight and vision, the superb thoughts and action, par excellence that could serve humanity and show practical ways of life and living, and the skill and ability for execution that has taught us that even a mighty sword has a limited movement but the pen of the writers, the tongue of the orators and the art of sculptors can very well command a world-wide movement; begin at last, to give way due to various reasons, poverty in most cases being the principal one. Their condition becomes precarious and at last, some die of starvation. They are forgotten or kept in oblivion, although the legacy they leave is immeasurable.

Can society look to this grave situation? Can the benevolent government and statesmen chalk out programmes for removing this serious blot and unwarranted sign of negation? Yes, they can. But sometimes they lack a sort of sympathy, imagination, great vision and elasticity in the choice of means, although ability propels them to do the needful. This is the panorama of the life of some of the great authors whose services to society are beyond imagination.

Under the circumstances, as detailed above, the entire issue of writers, authors, artists, musicians, singers and the like should be sympathetically, seriously, resourcefully, boldly and, above all, most effectively taken up with great vision lest—on account of the downfall of these neglected great personalities of the world—the perennial flow of the life of society be lagooned.

Education—Meaning and Definition

In Oriya (one of the constitutionally recognised languages of India) we use two words for education. They are *sikshya* and *bidya*. *Sikshya* is derived from the Sanskrit verb-root *sikh* meaning a disciplined study, and *bidya* from the verb root *bid*, which means 'to acquire knowledge'. In Sanskrit, we say, *sa bidya ja bimuktoye*. It means, 'that which liberates'. This—the educational philosophy of India—expresses that education means liberation—liberation of body, mind and spirit.

Some say that it is a preparation for life. Some say that what teaches us to be adaptable to varied circumstances of life is education. The generally acceptable definition is: "Education in its widest sense includes all the influences which act upon an individual during his passage from the cradle to the grave.

Let us take a look at the role and importance of education.

* In the case of an educated person, rationality dominates animality, while in the case of an illiterate person, animality dominates rationality. So, in ancient times, the Indian Aryans used to say, "devoid of education we are beasts."

- Education dispels ignorance, poverty and disease.

- An educated person depends a great deal on introspection, logic and reasoning. He tries to know himself first and then his neighbors. Socrates has said, 'Man, know thyself.'

- In 1993, a bench consisting of five judges of the Supreme Court of India observed that an educated citizen is a key to the growth and development of a country.

- Dayozelies, a great thinker, says, "The foundation of every state is the education of its youth."

- Keeping in view the pressing need of education in the world, the UNO introduced education for all in 1993.

- An educated and cultured brain is the cream of a nation.

- Education is an ornament to a nation.

- Education aims at the all-round development of man — physical, mental and spiritual.

- Education helps us to adapt ourselves to varied circumstances of life.

- In view of the importance of education, men of letters advise people to be students from their post-cradle to pre-grave life, as the courses of studies of the world university are never ending.

- Education polishes the brain, and the polished brain can draw philosophy from every nook and corner of society.

- Education develops international understanding and enriches our cosmic view.

- Education transforms man's personality.

- Man is a social animal and an educated man, being guided by reason, sincerely tries to construct society. Great writers, scholars, philosophers, social workers and statesmen are known for their noble deeds. It is because of their sincere efforts that society exists and grows.

- Education of good quality makes a good citizen. The growth of good citizens makes society rich and dynamic.

- In developing countries, education of women is the pressing need of the hour. Napoleon once said, "Give me good mothers and I will give you a good nation."

- Lack of education has increased the death rate of children.

- An educated and cultured society always tries to remove ignorance, poverty, disease, terrorism, indiscipline, insecurity of life, violence and war.

- Education embraces the golden rule, 'live and let live' and produces men of vision.

- Man, by nature, is a fighting animal. So, sound education alone can sublimate him.

- Education enables us to meet the challenges of life.

So how is it that the activities of some of the highly educated officers and others are detrimental to the interest of society and the country at large? This is rather unfortunate. All we can say is that they lack sound education, moral values and vision.

Problems of Education

Education is the basic need of society. The role of education, as mentioned above, is marvellous. Now some great thinkers of various fields are of the opinion that there is something wrong with the present system of education. Many education commissions and committees have been set up at different times to look into the problems of education and suggest measures for its improvement. But still, we have a long way to go.

In India, and in some of the third world countries, most people are illiterate. The question of universalisation of education was taken up in recent years. We spend less than three per cent of our gross domestic product on education, which should be at least six per cent. This we cannot do due to financial constraints. Extension of educational programme is unable to keep pace with the growth of population.

Some of the government officials have a lax attitude to educational development. Although the Constitution of India has made provision for universal education, education for all has not been possible due to lack of funds. The adult education and mass education programme has been at stake due to lack of sincere efforts. Also, we find deterioration in the quality of education, as more and more institutions are becoming commercial in nature and spirit.

The curricula, the syllabai, etc., are also defective. Frequent changes made in textbooks and curricula do not solve the problem. The authorities concerned prescribe more and more books even for lower classes. Students at English language schools look more like over-laden wageworkers than dedicated students. It is a pitiable sight. At times, students cannot follow the complexity of language because of their poor linguistic ability.

Inadequate and under-qualified staff (at some schools), lack of proper teaching aids, miserable condition of school buildings and shortage of furniture, etc., create a sorry picture. Teachers stay far from their schools, especially in rural areas. Some teachers are otherwise busy with earning more. Such teachers lack interest, sincerity and proficiency.

Nowadays schools and colleges have been broadly divided in two categories— one for the rich and the other for the poor. Children of the rich study in well-equipped private schools and colleges. Poor children go to ill-equipped government schools. After completion of their studies, rich students rise in life while poor students go down. Private educational institutions have become big business centres.

The education process and systems have undertaken a long exodus from ancient educational philosophers like Socrates, Plato and Aristotle and from the Gurukul system in India to education in modern times. Education today is highly specialised and, as such, rather expensive.

Solutions to the Problems

A new education policy has been adopted in India to improve the tone and tune of education. This policy makes us expect that the rate of literacy in the 15-35 age group will considerably rise in the near future. The policy of 1936 is an important landmark in the history of education in India. The salient features of this policy are as follows:

- Introduction of national core curriculum at school levels.

- Special attention to the education of women and the S.C./ S.T. people.

- Introduction of semester system at the secondary stage and examination reforms.

- Establishment of an all India educational service and pace-setting institutions called 'Navodaya Vidyalayas' in all parts of the country to provide equal opportunities—especially for students in rural areas—and to raise the quality of higher education.

- Delinking of jobs from degrees.

- Strengthening of the University Grants Commission, the All India Council of Technical Education, the India Council of Agricultural Research and the Indian Medical Council.

- Continuation of the 10 plus 2 plus 3 system of education.

- Splitting of 10 school years into an elementary system comprising five years followed by three years of middle school and two years of high school and provision of vocationalisation after the secondary stage. Students can take up the vocation of their choice at the end of their school education. This system would lead to 'the right boy in the right line'. This system has a sort of similarity with the concept of Mahatma Gandhi's basic education.

The Novodaya Vidyalays established in almost all the districts of our country is a right institution in the direction of introducing a uniform educational curriculum. These schools are well equipped in all respects. The Indira Gandhi National Open University is at work in the entire length and breadth of India.

The New Central Advisory Board of Education (CABE) is expected to solve the problems pertaining to the present examination systems that are giving sleepless nights to many students and inducing them to resort to mass copying, cheating and other such unwarranted activities in the examination hall.

Now Internet-based educational facilities on hundreds and thousands of websites are available throughout the world. Distant education is gaining ground even in developing countries.

Modern technology has now enabled students to take the cyberspace classroom.

Further Improvements

- Commissions and committees such as All India Council of Technical Education (AICTE) and the University Grants Commission (UGC) should be more independent and free from government control. Recognition should be granted only to well-equipped institutions.

- Government and private schools and colleges may concurrently run, but exercise of control over them should be a must. Now most of the government schools are being run without proper control. So quality education fails.

- All basic education should be nationalised so that all students—rich and poor—benefit equally.

- Rich students prefer to study at specialised colleges where expensive but better facilities are available. But while taking this advantage, institutions should not exploit students.

- A comprehensive system of education should be adopted at all levels in order to remove all defective elements in education. Universalisation of education (mass education) should be sincerely, resourcefully and effectively taken up.

- Students, their parents and teachers should join hands in achieving sound education.

- About one-third of our population is still illiterate. Most of them are very poor. So they neither have the willingness nor the ability to send their children to schools. Their pecuniary condition should be improved and adult education should be made effective.

- Now some schools have become sellers of education, and parents are the purchasers of it. It is a cold business.

- Teachers should be resourceful and responsible for the all round development of the student. It is said that 'a teacher enters the class, a good teacher enters the hearts of the students and a missionary teacher enters into the very life of the community'.

- A teacher should necessarily be a psychologist.

- Teachers should not engage themselves more in non-educational activities than in activities related to the education of their students.

- They should try their best to put students in the place of discoverers.

- Teaching of secularism, touchability, patriotism, etc., should never be disregarded.

- In underdeveloped and developing countries, education has failed to thrive fully—especially in the Adivasi and remote areas. Measures like 'surprise visits', 'no work, no pay', etc., may check defaulters.

- Nowadays some students have become rather irresponsible and undisciplined. The authorities concerned should carefully, tactfully and resourcefully deal with this issue.

- Today's education is rather job-oriented. Knowledge of Ethics does not matter much. Those who fail to get jobs resort to antisocial activities. So education should be tempered with moral education.

- Syllabus should be designed to suit the sights and sounds and vision of the present century. Science and technology, computer science, space education, audio-visual aids, environment studies, Internet-based education, arts and architecture, sculpture, horse riding, swimming, mountaineering and futurity of the universe should figure in the syllabai.

- Books fairs should be given a lot of importance.

- Reading habit should be encouraged. It is said that 'if you want to talk to the super brain, go through the books'.

- G. K. Chesterton says, "A house without a book is as good as a body without soul."

- The creation theory should be taught at schools and colleges. This should figure in the first chapters of subjects such as Geography, Science and History; then other theories—such as the formation theory—may follow. According to the formation theory, the earth was formed by a mass falling off the sun. The creation theory affirms that God created the universe. This is necessary if the idea of God is to be entertained.

Human Resource Development

What is human resource development? It is about developing the capabilities that are latent and potent in every citizen to the fullest extent. The people of a particular country are the real asset of that country. They find ways of prosperity. History records human achievements in various fields. For example, Germany and Japan were shattered during the Second World War, but they successfully developed their human resources to become strong nations again. Mishandling of manpower or improper utilisation of human resources is one of the main reasons of the downfall of a nation.

Health and education are more important than land, money and such other things. Suffering and inefficiency are caused by ill health. A sick person may lose employment.

Diversion of all our resources to the eradication of poverty, disease and ignorance is the pressing need of the hour. If you want to rapidly develop human resources, you will be required to make necessary arrangement for training your people to use manpower properly. We have abundant manpower but we have been, so far, unable to utilise it properly. If human resources are developed first and properly utilized, we can have marvellous achievements in various fields. Well-organised and developed human resources contribute a lot towards the formation of a better state.

Realising the gravity of this issue, the government of India set up a ministry for the purpose of human resource development. It is very much hoped that this ministry will work with all sympathy, imagination, vision and elasticity in the choice of means.

CHAPTER VI

Sociology

Auguste Comte, the founding father of sociology, defines sociology as the science of social phenomena 'subject to natural and invariable laws, the discovery of which is the object of investigation'. Emile Durkheim, Alex Lukles, Harry M Johson, Kimball Young, Raymond W. Mack and Kingsley Davis also define 'sociology' in their own ways. Morris Ginsberg says, "In the broadest sense, sociology is the study of human interactions and inter-relations, their conditions and consequences." Scholars say that sociologists express different opinions in the matter of definitions. Of course, the idea of 'man and society' is common in their definitions, which is important. We may define sociology as follows: "Sociology is the scientific study of the origin of man, development of societies and human behavior in groups."

There are quite a few theories of the origin of society. Some of them are discussed below. The propounders of these theories try to illustrate the origin of society, but they do not touch upon the question of the origin of man.

Divine Theory

This theory expounds that society is a creation of God. Although it is true, some sociologists and historians do not believe it. They say that it has no scientific and rational basis, etc. Interestingly, even the divine theory does not touch upon the creation of man. It is surprising to note that man does not distinctly appear on the stage of sociology. Who came first—man or society? It is a sort of revolving round the pivot of the origin of eggs, their hatching into chicks, etc. We are not looking for the 'bird'. One should know that society is composed of men and not vice-versa. So the origin of man should be traced first. This is imperative and vital. Society did not fall from a flying disc nor did it emerge from some deep den.

Theory of Force

According to this theory, the strong ruled over the weak. Where did the strong come from? No answer. The strong should come first; their origin, nativity, etc., should be ascertained first. This point (creation of man) is the nerve centre of sociology.

Social Contract Theory

This theory states that men lived originally in a "state of nature". Again we find the same confusion. Where did the man who was in a state of nature come from? No answer.

Sociologists differ from one another in the subject matter of this theory.

Patriarchal Theory

This theory explains that society owes its origin to the family. It does not say anything about the origin of the father (man) and the other members. One may argue that this father in question comes from his father and so on. Then what about the origin of the first father (man) who appeared on earth? No answer.

Matriarchal Theory

This theory says that society originated from the matriarchal family. This theory is also silent about the present issue.

Evolutionary Theory

This theory almost condemns all the other theories mentioned above and expounds that society is a product of a long and slow process of evolution.

Evolution can never form or create anything on earth. First of all, the soil (to hold water), the water and the jellyfish should be created. Then alone one may think of evolution, which is speculative. The aforesaid organic and non-organic things should be created first, as they can never evolve themselves into different species. Some social thinkers, without attempting to prove the origin of man historically, logically, rationally and, above all, scientifically, say that man is a social animal. It is true, but what about the origin of man? It is always imperative to know the first and the foremost grandfather of ours.

Thanks to Auguste Comte who, finally, comes forward with certain logic, reasoning and conviction to indicate our perversion, malobservation, wrong perception and misconception and diffuse the glow of "theological thoughts" in order to dispel darkness in which we were groping all along. What is theology? The word 'theology' comes from the Greek word 'theologia'. It means, 'discourse on God'. It is a serious piece of writing about God. It further means the study of religions, religious ideas and beliefs. It is connected with the creed and the dogma of different religions. In short, it is about knowing one's self and God and understanding the establishment of the holy communion of man with God.

Comte divides theological stages into three sub-stages:

1. Fetishism,
2. Polytheism
3. Monotheism

The fetish is an object. People believed that this object possessed some spiritual power, which could do good and bad things. They tried to use evil power against their enemies. The primitive men believed that objects like some wood, bones, stones, etc., contained this power, which could do miracles. They developed this thought and could enter into the second stage of theological thinking. This was called polytheism. Polytheism means belief in many gods and goddesses. Now let us come to the third stage, which is known as monotheism. It proclaims the supremacy of one God. He is omnipotent, omniscient and omnipresent. He has created animate beings and all things. He says, "Apart from me there is no liberator. When I act who can reverse it?" One can never measure the mysteries of God. He has created all things including man.

Great thinkers, religious philosophers, eminent scholars, super scientists and the leading theologians of the world have already conclusively proved that the first man on earth was the handiwork of God. Sociology, without the scientific description of the origin of man, is something like an autobiography without the name of parents, the date and place of birth, etc., of the writer of the autobiography.

Again, let us come to our first question as to who is the first and the foremost grandfather of ours in order to conclude this subject matter. Any humble attempt to trace him out is not only the question of burning curiosity, but of paramount importance. When the divine theory, the third theological theory and the creation theory (not the formation theory, by-chance theory or the "origin of species", etc.) are combinedly and scientifically studied with all logic and reasoning, then alone can one find the first man. It can be accepted, at least, for the time being without groping here and there until the truth, the only truth, if any, in matter of the origin of man is discovered. Let the scientific investigation in the matter run fast.

Sociology without illustrations relating to the origin of man loses its connotation and intrinsic value. Now the descended of the fourth man created by God is performing marvellous deeds in the world, and the very cock and hen that were all along in oblivion are found in the arena of sociology. So one can now conduct thorough researches on eggs, chicks and the cocks that can very well use the 'theory of force' in a cock-pit crowing 'cock-a-doodle doo' and form a society of fowls.

CHAPTER VII

Transformation

What is transformation? It is a change completely in form, appearance, nature, behavior, etc. It has more of spiritual value than the temporal one, unlike 'social development'. The word *transformation* is deeply connected with the all-round development of society, viz. physical, mental and spiritual development. We call it liberation of body, liberation of mind and liberation of spirit. The thoughts and actions of super statesmen are solely meant for this transformation.

Today, the state has become the guardian of its citizen. It takes multipurpose projects in order to remove poverty, food problems, etc. It gives all attention to provide shelter, clothing, health care, education, communication and irrigation facilities and meets all the other needs. Some of the private organisations come forward to help the state in the matter of transformation of society. Then what do the citizens do? Do they sit tight and eat foods supplied by the state. No. The people elect their representatives who form the government. All the citizens have great responsibilities. If citizens are good, society becomes good. Selfishness, dishonesty, malpractices, etc., should not exist in society. All the citizens should be conscious of their privileges and responsibilities.

Sometimes the citizens think that their responsibility is much more than the privilege they get from the state. They think that some are paying heavy taxes to the government. They should know that what they are paying towards taxes and other duties has 'no quid pro quo' with the privilege. It means that it has no par with the privilege we enjoy. For example, the private bus-owner runs his bus along the road constructed by the State and earns a lot of money. Now had there been no road, he could not have constructed even 5 kms. of road for his bus. So, what all he pays as road tax, etc., is quite meagre in comparison to the huge amount of income from bus service. His responsibility in the State is that he should accept the principle of the minimum travel charge system. This example is analogous to every sphere of activity. Citizens have the responsibility of causing no harm in any way to national or private property. This is, in short, the privileges and responsibility of a citizen. This is the working of a democratic set-up in a welfare state.

Mass-cooperation, honest discharge of duties and wholehearted response of citizens are highly necessary for an ideal State. Therefore, all evil practices must disappear from society. "Work I must for the common weal should be each and every one's zeal." With these few words of democratic thoughts and actions, let us proceed with the subject matter. We have already said a word about physical, mental and spiritual transformation. Our approach to the subject is very simple but forceful and effective. Now, our transformation touches all classes of people including Dalits. First of all, let us come to physical transformation.

Physical Transformation
Food, water, agriculture, clothing shelter, health care, etc., fall into this category.

Food

Food is the most basic need of all living beings. The moment a child is born, it cries out for food. Napoleon, once said, "Give them food and lead them anywhere you like." A hungry man cannot pay attention to anything but food. And, unfortunately, most of the third world countries are suffering because of want of food. In 1866, famine played havoc in Orissa. Some of the people of Koraput district lived on fruits, roots and leaves during the famine.

During pre-independent time, it was seen and felt that most of the people living in the undivided Koreput district of Orissa used to eat only 'raggi-gruel' with curry as their lunch. They used to take some rice at night. This was a very common feature then. Even today this condition prevails in some of the families. It is a very pitiable and challenging situation, especially in the 21st century.

Let us illustrate one of the funny but noble deeds of one of our writers who were about six years old then. He used to take the share of his rice from his mother to a poor boy's home. This poor boy used to bring his gruel. They used to eat the rice as well as the gruel together. This arrangement continued for a few days. Then it automatically discontinued—perhaps due to household interference. The poor boy, now a poor man, is still alive in a remote village. We know that food problems arise on account of less production, growth of population, natural calamities, ignorance in the matter of livelihood, idleness, bad practice like resorting to alcoholic drinks and gambling, etc. Here let us narrate a funny but painful incident that took place in a village. The wife of a drunkard put some paddy in a big basket and got it covered with hay and mud with a view to utilising it during the next rainy days. On discovery, the drunkard broke the cover, took out the entire paddy, filled the basket with husks and covered it as his wife had previously done. Now he sold the paddy and helped himself with liquor for a few days. The wife discovered the fraud only during the rainy season. The whole family had to suffer during the rainy season. People such as the drunkard in question have no present, no future.

The following brief statistics will give a picture of acute food problem of the world including India. The Food and Agriculture Organisation of the UNO reports that about 81 crore people of the poor countries the world over go to bed without food. About one-third of the entire population of India lives on half meals and about 20 crore people take malnutritious food. About 35 crore people are below the poverty line and about 70 million children of India die for want of food. About 51 per cent of people of the rural areas and 39 per cent of the people living in urban areas do not get nutritious foods. In Orissa, 56 per cent of the people living in rural areas and about 46 per cent of the people living in urban areas do not get nutritious food. Recently, in the monsoon session (on 18/8/05) of the council of states of the Indian parliament, there was a hot discussion over the problem of acute shortage of food, clothes and shelter, etc. The foremost duty of the government is to remove hunger from the face of the country.

Growth of Population

It is also one of the burning problems. The Registrar General of India has recently published information relating to the population projection of India wherein he states that in 1996 the population was 93.4 crores and this number will increase to 126.4 crores in 2016. Just after the partition of India, the population was 34.2 crores. Now it is more than 110 crores. The Registrar cautioned us saying that the population will be 216 crores by 2050. This is the magnitude of the problem.

Problems pertaining to distribution of food products, communication, ignorance including illiteracy of women and bad practices, etc., should be solved keeping in view the suggestions of experts. Suggestions relating to illiteracy, bad practices, etc., have been made in different chapters.

Let us try to solve the problems. Poverty is a challenge to human intellect. We have to meet this challenge. Recently, the present United Progressive Government of India made provision in law that the government will provide work at least to one person of a family for one hundred days in a year at Rs. 60 per day and the other members who go without work will get some compensation. Women will receive special treatment in the matter.

Agriculture
Agriculture needs special attention.

- It is agriculture that can remove hunger and poverty from the world. So under no circumstances agricultural reforms can be neglected. Investment of money, irrigation, distribution of food grains, communication and supply of good seeds, effective insecticide, manures and such other things should be emphasised.

- Experts should be pressed into research work that will go to different areas of different climatic conditions and carry on research work in that area. They will also suggest how to improve the condition of agriculture even in areas damaged by natural calamities.

- We should pay attention to rotation of crops, application of natural manures and intensive cultivation and co-operative farming, etc.

- The production of agricultural goods should keep pace with the growth of population. Growth of population is a problem. So it should be checked.

- Irrigation facilities should be extended to remote areas.

- Division of big plots into several small ones should be discouraged. Contraction of cultivable lands due to rapid growth of industries, deforestation, etc., are dangerous signs for agricultural development.

- Different types of interest-free loans should be floated; this measure would stop farmers from committing suicide due to non-payment of government loan. Top priority should be given to the well-being of the farmer Let the following be the maxim: 'Anger the farmers, hunger for food.'

- Principal food grains and economic crops should be simultaneously produced to meet basic needs.

- In many parts of our country, poor people get work in agricultural firms for about six months and for the rest six months they go without work, which causes them to suffer from want of food. They should be otherwise engaged in constructive work like making roads, railways, houses for the poor and the like.

- Cold storage systems for the preservation of food materials should be reorganised in the most up-to-date scientific ways.

- Helicopters should be pressed into services for irrigating the most fertile areas in highlands where adoption of any other irrigation system is not possible. We will effectively think of causing artificial rain.

- Joining of rivers, deepening of them and removal of mud, etc., from the riverbeds and such other related works should be taken up on war footing. Of course, joining of rivers, etc., may lead to provincial, national and international problems in the near future.

- Deserts can be irrigated by waters brought through pipe lines.

- Sea and lake-waters should be scientifically used.

- Different types of wells may be dug up keeping the water level, climatic conditions, etc., in view. All these things would go a long way towards solving the drinking water problem.

- Works related to exports and imports and globalisation, including protection by patent of food grains, may be taken up.

- The present food supply systems should be organised on war footing and more sincere people should be appointed to do the needful.

- In third world countries, many children die of malnutrition. Recently, Mr. Michael Diamond, Asia Director of one of the international organisations called PLAN, observed that about sixty crore children of Asia are poverty-stricken. Their condition is precarious (*The Samaya* dated 26/08/2005, p3). They and expectant mothers should be provided with balanced nutrition. Of course, as some say, these things are not new. Then how is it that all these problems do not disappear from the scene? It is unfortunate. We must consider these problems and see to it that all the ill effects are totally removed.

Growth of Population

- Most people cannot afford entertainment because of poverty. So they spend much of their time in sexual activity at home. Such people normally produce children like rabbits.

- Many people are ignorant of the devastating effect of the rapid growth of population.

- Most people want sons as they believe that only sons should set fire to the funeral pyre of their parents. The question of preservation of dynasty, old age and security problems, etc., encourage the growth of population.

- Some minority communities welcome the growth of population because they are scared of the political situation; they just want to grow in number.

Ignorance should be removed by making people understand the gravity of the situation. Self-control, use of contraceptives, etc., will help solve problems. Some people try to give expert suggestions saying that Malthusian Theory of Population will be in operation. Natural calamities like flood, storms, famine, disease, eruptions of volcanoes, etc., will take the lives of hundred and thousand of people within a few minutes and thus a sort of balance in the growth of population would be maintained.

Some people present religious views saying that God knows the consequences and solves the problems in question. These two concepts also appear to be reasonable and acceptable from many points of view. However, the growth of population should be checked in natural ways observing all ethical and spiritual principles.

Removal of food problems and poverty comes within the purview of agriculture, industrialisation, technological education, exports and imports systems, employment, population, communication, natural calamities, economic development, globalisation, political willingness, etc. Let us take a look at these issues.

Dwelling Houses and Shelters

Amongst the three requirements for man, namely food, clothes and shelter, shelter is perhaps the most important. The first question we normally ask after a long journey is, 'Where to stay'. Some consider food as the most important requirement for man while others attach importance to clothes. Still others gave the greatest importance to shelter. If you have no place to put your two legs what will you do?

History says that primitive people lived in caves. Even now quite a few live in wooden cabins, by canals and railway sides, at railway stations and in deserted places. Some people live in palatial buildings while others have no houses to live in. The 2001 census points out that there are about 78 million homeless people in India now. Due to population explosion, people are becoming poorer and poorer. Some villagers have no food, no clothes and no houses to live in. So they run to towns and cities to earn their livelihood. There they live in miserable slums.

One of our authors was going to Guwahati, Assam, by train. The train stopped for some time near the Guwahati railway station in the afternoon. The station was centrally located in the city. So he was surprised to see a slum in such a place. Rehabilitation of slum dwellers is a must. But it should be done with proper care and sympathy.

India is in need of 19.3 million houses (12.70 million in rural areas and 6.6 million in urban areas). During 2001-02, around 1, 25,000 crores were spent on the construction of houses for the homeless. But a lot still needs to be done. (The statistics given here and there may be outdated due to the late publication of the book.)

The following steps should be taken to solve this problem:

- Correct information about the homeless should be obtained. Often we find undeserving people getting houses under different government schemes.

- Different types of loans on quite a reasonable interest should be granted to the poor and the homeless for construction of houses.

- Allotment of 400 decimal of site to each deserving family is to be encouraged.

- Engineers may be directed to teach people how to construct houses with latrines at a cheaper rate.

- Materials for houses should be provided to the homeless at a cheaper rate.

- The town planning office should be sincere and helpful in sanctioning house plan easily and without delay.

- Land settlement affairs and the issue of pattas should be handled diligently.

- Growth of population and intrusion by people should be effectively checked.

- Displaced persons should be rehabilitated in suitable places without delay.

- Psychological treatment is necessary for those who leave their native environments.

- Many villagers live in huts unsuitable for human inhabitation; measures should be taken to improve the quality of their dwelling places.

- Some people build grand houses. Then they bequeath them to their sons. Gradually, these houses become dilapidated due to lack of proper care and maintenance. Efforts should be made to improve the condition of such houses as well.

Clothes

Cotton is widely used in India for clothing. India has been cultivating cotton since time immemorial. But more attention should be given to the cultivation of cotton and development of cotton industries. The wool and silk industries should also be developed.

Clothes should be available at much cheaper rate. The rich should be encouraged to donate clothes to the poor. Cloth shop owners should also be encouraged to donate clothes to the needy. On December 25, 2002, one of our authors donated 55 blouse pieces to each housewife of a particular village; he also gave sweets to some villagers. Such ways and means should be sought till the condition improves. Besides this, the task of feeding the hungry and healing the sick should be taken up diligently.

Time and Change

The beginning and the end of time is not within the knowledge of man. It is eternal in nature. So it is called "Mahakala", the great time. It runs like a highway. It does not enter into any house. Just as we channel water from the main canal, so also we are to bring the current from the great source of time. If we use it properly; we will prosper.

Time has nothing to do with change. Keep time away from the stages of the growth of a boy and see what happens. The boy grows, fruit ripen, seasons change. So if time is not responsible for change, then what is responsible for it? The environment, situations and circumstances, conditions, positions, geographical influences and the like change. We measure the period of a situation, geographical influence, etc., with the unit of time. So, changes are brought about not by time, but by the passage of time.

Old-age Problems and Solutions

Old age is a major problem. There is an Oriya saying about it. Just as the teeth do not like 'Khoda' (a kind of tasty vegetable-plant, the fibres of which stick into the teeth.), so also householders do not like a 'budha' (an old man).

The following are the main old-age problems:

- Old people are physically and mentally old and feeble; so people regard them a burden. They are, therefore, neglected.

- Old people normally have toilet-related problems; so taking care of them could be rather troublesome.

- Some might be deaf, dumb or otherwise disabled.
- Their solitary life is painful for them.
- Poverty makes old-age care more problematic.
- Some old people are compelled by their circumstances to work till their very end.
- Some age rapidly due to various reasons.
- Sometimes we find mournful expressions on their faces; some of them are terribly afraid of death.
- They want to fly like a bird but their body does not allow them to do so; they are sort of 'caged'.
- As their acquaintances and relatives are very much busy with their lives in general, they feel very lonely at times.
- Their grandchildren hardly give them attention.
- Some old people pre-maturely suffer due to their past undisciplined lives.
- Some old persons gradually lose interest in life and society; they become rather miserly and peevish.

Solutions
- Old age does not commonly touch all alike with its mighty hands with the same force and strength. So try to lead a decent life even in old age.
- *Brahmacharis* (searcher after the truth) and those who lead a disciplined life during their youth lead a happy life in old age.
- Save money for the future. Do not be a miser but cultivate frugal habits.
- Try to maintain good health; try to be free from tension and worry.
- Fear not death, as it is a part of God's plan.

- Take remedial measures from time to time. By virtue of your resourcefulness enable the householders to find ways and means of raising funds for medical treatment, etc.

- Control your anger; let your mind dwell on things spiritual.

- Old people should try to keep themselves busy; they should spend their time on reading, writing, visiting friends and relatives, playing with their grandchildren, etc. If they are strong enough, they should help the helpless.

- The young must take care of their aged parents. They should go out of their way to keep them clean and happy.

- One of our writers wrote:

  Old age is a comfortable cage
  If it attains the quality of a sage,
  Do good to others for all ages
  And brighten all life-pages.

What a valuable piece of advice!

- Old care centres, asylums, ashrams, etc., for the old should be developed further.

- One should try to donate food, clothes etc., to the old and old care centres.

The task of economical development and improvement of the condition of health and hygiene and other matters pertaining to physical transformation will be diligently undertaken by us.

Ethical Transformation

Ethical transformation is also known as moral transformation. Ethics is the science of morality. Physical transformation is mainly concerned with the outer development of man, while moral transformation is deeply connected with the inner values of life. It refers to all the good qualities of man. Let us consider one of the good qualities—character.

Character

Our behaviour and manners express our personality and character. Honesty, compassion, morality, truthfulness, discipline, good manners, courtesy, gentleness, friendship, self-reliance, introspection, etc., are part of character.

Character is something like an ever-burning light that dispels the darkness of immorality. Without it life would be charmless. It directs the course of our fortune. It is the centre of peace, good health, success, beauty and grace. It is a rare and precious quality.

The young should cultivate good character. If you go through the biographies of great personalities, you will find they were people of high character.

Character building has an important role to play in the development of human civilisation. Mahatma Gandhi said, "Any science that does not help build up character is no science at all."

Spiritual Transformation

Religion is a way of life that leads to God. It comes within the purview of the spiritual triangle—religion, God and man. God is the centre of the triangle. Without Him religion has no meaning, no entity. He leads man to Him through religion, scriptures preceptors, faith, conversion and the like. He liberates man from his physical, mental and spiritual bondages. Prayer and meditation are the means through which one can have deep connection with God. Prayer is the spiritual process of establishing Holy Communion with God. When a man is free from spiritual bondage, he becomes a spiritual man. This is called spiritual transformation. In order to be a spiritual man, one should embrace God.

Conversion

Conversion is change of faith, religious rites, etc. The history of religions indicates that many wars have been fought for religion, conversion being the main reason for them. Conversion should not be carried out through force, as it is a matter of change of heart. Religion should aim at inner transformation. You cannot teach/preach anything to a hungry man. Love him, serve him first. Mahatma Gandhi said, "What higher aim one can attain than to relieve human pain." Conversion should not entail jealousy, misconceptions, misunderstandings, hatred and violence. We should also note: 'Prayer changes things.'

〜

CHAPTER VIII

Aspects of Political Affairs

Democracy is a form of political set-up in which the people of a nation exercise equal control over the matters that affect their interests. In political organisations such as autocracy, dictatorship, theocracy and oligarchy, the basic rights of common citizens are not entertained.

Merits of Democracy

- Democracy provides sufficient scope for the all-round development of a citizen.

- A citizen has the right to speech, etc.

- All are equal before the eye of law.

- Of course, there are various inequalities in matters such as morality, lifestyles, physical and mental capacities and so on.

- Democracy implies discipline, mutual respect, etc.

- Democracy gives ample chance of growing one's leadership; all get the chance of becoming a leader on merit.

- The opposition plays an important role in democracy; it is the guiding factor of government. In the British Parliament, the opposition is officially recognised as His Majesty's opposition.

- Democracy aims at the welfare of the masses.

- The parliamentary system of government works smoothly if there are two main political parties. In such a case, a strong tug of war would exists between the minority and the majority. This position makes the government active in all respects.

- In a democratic set-up, public opinion is held in high esteem. The press and other forms of media have a vital role to play in democracy.

Demerits

- If people are influenced by communalism and money, democracy would assume an odd colour.

- On account of mass illiteracy, as in India, the media lose its effectiveness. As a result, illiterate people are manipulated by politicians.

- Sometimes, those who know very little of politics are elected by the ignorant masses.

- Sometimes, poverty, threats, etc., compel voters to make the wrong choices.

- Party politics and selfishness are bad for democracy.

- Internal quarrels, lust for power, etc., are bad signs.

- Regional political parties may create national disunity.

- Malafide treatment to the opposition hampers the day-to-day affairs of government.

Political Reformations

- Violent demonstrations, outcry, violence, etc., during the time of election propaganda should be checked.

- There should be two are three political parties.

- The ruling party should strengthen the opposition.

- The opposition should be constructive in its activities. It should guide the ruling party in the matter of efficient administration.

- The councilors, ward members and presidents of village panchayats and others can easily identify the voters in their own area. If anything goes wrong, they may be held responsible for it.

- Voters should not be indifferent to polling. However, those of the voters who are seriously ill or deeply engaged in some urgent and important piece of work may not go to cast their votes. Some of the voters are fed up with the undesirable activities of their representatives. So they do not want to exercise their franchise. In such an event, the candidate may again win the election taking advantage of the absence of the voters of a particular area. These dejected people may vote in favour of the suitable candidate and get him or her elected.

- Some unworthy candidates may win the election under the influence of the party's symbol. Generally, such candidates do not actively involve themselves in development work on account of their indifference and unworthiness. This point should not be lost sight of.

- In some undeveloped areas, only the same candidates may get elected again and again, as there may not be other better candidates. The government must develop such areas.

- Awareness-building centres should be organised to improve the tones and tunes, sights and sounds, vision and insights of the people. Literacy programmes should be diligently taken up; poverty should be checked on war footing.

- Assessment of the political career and day-to-day activities of the members of different political institutions should be made from time to time.

- Sometimes the face value may work and not the intrinsic value of good suggestions made by some of the members; it should be avoided.

- Indifference of members to any decisions is totally harmful to the nation.

- Idleness, muteness, indifference, etc., should be discouraged. Once the members of a particular executive body were discussing the abolition of a particular organisation. Some of the members were dozing while others were not interested in the discussion. A few were expressing jarring opinions. Knowing and feeling the gravity of the situation, some responsible persons, including one of the writers of the book, entered the meeting hall with due permission and, by virtue of their skillful presentation of facts and arguments, created a very colourful and sensational atmosphere in it. They changed the whole situation. The organisation could thrive and fared well. It may be analogous to the affairs of some of the members of the political organisations.

- Absence of members in the sessions of different councils and parliament should be checked. They should act as the best goalkeepers. Decisions that are detrimental to the interest of the country should not be passed.

- Age, health and qualification of candidates should be taken into account. Old and feeble persons suffering from chronic diseases should not take active part in politics. However, their wisdom and experiences may be inherited and used.

- They should be free from communalism and colour prejudice.

- Refresher courses should be organised for the members in order to make them more efficient parliamentarians.

- Well-argued speeches, a lively and constructive debate and all good deeds should be rewarded.

- Giving or taking bribes, if any, should be discouraged.

- Voters should not resort to meanness like voting in other's name, capturing polling stations and vote boxes, etc.

- The voters, the candidates and the members (already elected) should follow the code of conduct framed for the whole purpose.

- Voters should learn to be conscious of their franchise; they should remain far from undesirable influences.

- Candidates or members should dedicate themselves to the cause of the nation; they should have social conscience.

- They should always dream of super democracy.

- Each of them should be a statesman.

- They should try to unite people without hurting their religious feelings and maintain secularism in the true sense of the term; they should give top priority to social and economic problems.

- They should not take advantage of the political illiteracy of the people.

Women Candidates

Some women have proved themselves to be very good administrators and parliamentarians, so they should be encouraged to contest elections. Provision should be made for their easy entry into assemblies and parliaments. Reservation of seats will help them to enter into politics. Some of the women possessing all the right qualifications to be good parliamentarians may be taken on a selection basis, which should be more elastic than the present nomination system.

Emergency

Sometimes, *emergency* is imposed on the people. It is a constitutional provision. When indiscipline, chaos, confusion, lawlessness and so on raise their ugly heads in a country, emergency appears with a gay spirit to stabilise democracy. So it is a super democracy. Some people cannot understand the value of it. It is the duty of the super statesmen who are in charge of the state of affairs of a country to run the administration during the emergency period in accordance with the welfare code and in consultations with experts.

If the majority is formed by good members and 'Super Beings' in the political institution, there will be no serious problems in the country. Our Super Beings can effectively manage the affairs of the country.

United Nations Organisation

The role of the United Nations Organisation in the matter of peace, which is its foremost aim, has been remarkable. It also focuses on the following objectives: removing threats of war from the world, establishing brotherhood and better understanding among the nations, looking into the economic development of different countries and undertaking the task of social transformation and settling disputes.

The UNO has six main departments: the International Court of Justice, the Secretariat, the General Assembly, the Security Council, the Economic Council and the Social Council. All the countries of the world can be members of the General Assembly. It sits once a year. All the problems of different countries are solved here, but the pity is that the decision of this Assembly is not binding on any country. They may or may not follow the decision, but the Security Council is very powerful. Some of the powerful countries are members of this council. The USA, Russia, Britain, France and China are members of this council. Now India is trying to be a member of this council. The members of the Security Council have 'Veto' power. By virtue of this power, these countries can make the decisions of the UNO ineffective. Even the resolutions of the Security Council become ineffective on account of the use of such 'Vetos'. There are six countries that are temporary members of this council. The Council can take up matters pertaining to atom bombs, education, health, wars, etc. The International Court of Justice consists of as many as 15 judges. There are sub departments in the UNO. They are International Labour Organisation (LO), Food and Agriculture Organisation (FAQ), United National Economic, Social and Cultural Organisation (UNESCO), World Health Organisation (WHO), World Bank, etc. The member countries bear the expenses of the UNO. The blue flag of this organisation symbolises peace, fraternity and unity.

The role of the UNO in the context of averting war and settling disputes has been remarkable. It has diligently taken up the problems of Israel and Palestine, Berlin, Korea, Vietnam, Libya and Iran. It is also attempting to solve some burning issues, such as the Kashmir issue, the boundary issues of India and many other issues.

The UNO is a democratic organisation. It proclaims the democratic dogma to the whole world. Such a great organization should enjoy enormous powers in order to control international tensions. Many poor and weak countries solely depend on this organisation. But because of political interference of some powerful countries it cannot satisfactorily help the helpless. So, at times, the very purpose of the UNO is defeated. So it is the bounded duty of every member country to strengthen this organisation, to make it supreme and magnificent in all respects and to get all the privileges out of it. If the UNO is legally and democratically protected, it will protect the whole world.

CHAPTER IX

Aspects of General Administration

A dministration is management of the affairs of government for the welfare of the people. It is a system of the security of society. Prosperity, social progress and peace fully depend upon the administrative system of the State.

We know that administration should aim at the all-round development of the country. Development depends on roadways, railways, industries, agriculture, science and technology and so on. Besides this, there is a very peculiar, curious and amazing way of rapidly developing a country. A country would develop overnight if bribery and corruptions were checked. This single-sentence statement needs vivid and graphic descriptions. This account of bribes, corruption, etc., is fiction. In a few cases, some of these points may be true. Now let us enter into the fiction. Let us start from the Education Department of our imaginary country. Bribery has gained access to this department. In some educational institutions, money is illegally collected at the time of admission of students. Some of the poor and weak students are scared of bad teachers, who, with a view to extract money, force them to attend private classes. Had the teacher been sincere in the class, the poor parents would have saved the tuition money. In some institutions, scholarships are misappropriated. Many students are resorting to malpractice beginning from passing examinations to procuring academic certificates. Even highly 'educated' college teachers are adopting various undesirable ways and means to go abroad for Ph.D. degrees and flattering authorities for promotion and so on. Undervaluation of answer books is leading to suicide (in a few cases).

A poor farmer or a fourth-class government servant gets his children educated by spending his hard-earned money. It is painful to him. But that is not the end of the story, for he has to bribe the concerned authorities in order to get jobs for them. To get one's work done in a government office, one has to grease the palm of the concerned official. If he has to get his daughter married, he has to give a handsome dowry to the bridegroom or members of his family. Dowry is also a big social menace. Bribery and the dowry system stymie modernization. The dowry system is one of the main causes that encourage bribery

Now let us imagine a murder case. There are varied reasons for committing murder. A rich man may engage miscreants to kill a poor man in order to take his piece of land or something. They murder the man, bribe some officials and escape from punishment. The family of the murdered man weeps not only for the death, but also for the false postmortem report. The parents of the murdered man might have spent some money at the hospital at the time of his birth. During his lifetime he may have spent some money illegally to get his various works done, as narrated above; thus the man (the murdered one) was born at the hospital through bribery, led his life through bribery and embraced death through bribery. What a terrible and piteous story! The blood of the man so murdered cries out to God from the grave. Those who took bribe will surely be under the curse of the Supreme. Such inhumane incidents take place every day in our imaginary country. These gruesome events may be a matter of imagination but they may be true in reality. The god-sent punishment would be inevitable. Our newspapers are full of reports of theft, murder, rape, bribery, etc. Some of the administrators concerned are almost silent, as if they have no information of these things. Of course, culprits are caught and punished. But it is like a drop in the ocean. Most of them escape from the clutches of law through bribery.

In our realm of imagination curious incidents take place. Let us consider another example. Some country liquor sellers bribe the excise department and safely carry on their business (adulterated liquor). Some such culprits are punished at times. The lower-level employees try to prove some cases in the Court of Law so that the culprits would be punished. All this is to show that employees are not silent over any such crimes. In some cases, the employees concerned encourage the thieves, who give them a good amount of money and articles, to be successful in their trade. In such events, the rich become poor overnight on account of theft. Sometimes, innocent persons are punished while culprits escape due to deliberate negligence of duty. Sometimes insincerity and inefficiency give rise to unpleasant events. Let us consider a funny incident: Once the police were taking a thief to the court of law for a trial. Finding an opportunity, the thief ran away from the policemen. Being helpless and scared of the consequences, they caught hold of an innocent man who was going to a weekly market. He was presented to the court for a trial. As he knew nothing of the theft, he could not say anything about it. The judge was a very resourceful and judicious gentleman. So, he could readily grasp the entire situation correctly and let lose the innocent man and then imposed punishment on the policemen.

Now let us consider the elected personalities. Most of them are not free from corruption. They are not statesmen. The other day some good persons were discussing the misappropriation of public funds by some elected persons of high rank. One of the gentlemen remarked that even legally earned money could not be fully spent by the elected persons. So was the opportunity for them. He added in amazement that in such favourable situations how could they come forward to touch public funds? Ah! the desire of the flesh is never-ending. Some of the MLAs and MPs in our realm are not free from murder and rape cases. Some are indifferent to food adulteration, which is so crucial in human life, Apart from this corruption, there are different kinds of scams. If some corrupt administrators, officers and ministers are asked to deliver a speech on morality, discipline and corruption, they will keep the audience spell-bound. The language, the style, the movement, the faces and visage—all are attractive to the core. Someone remarked that such politicians should be called 'dove-feathered ravens' or 'wolves in lamb's guise'. The only reason for this corruption is that their selfish desires do not allow them to do good things in life. In our realm of imagination, some policemen and clerks are the pivots round which the wheels of corruption revolve.

Thus, one will find that almost every citizen is losing money on account of illegal payment for each and every piece of work done for him, beginning from a small amount to the tune of several thousands of rupees which has to be kept on a par with the nature of crimes, works, etc. If bribery is checked, various kinds of taxes are properly collected, vigilance authorities are strengthened and powers are sincerely delegated to them for recovery of the illegally earned money from corrupt employees and if such other related works as these are diligently taken up will not the country be rich overnight? Checking bribery has no meaning unless and until it is tempered with orders to the concerned officers or clerks to do what is right on time.

This is the panorama of the life in the imaginary corrupt country that has been presented here as fiction. Now it is up to the people to study, examine and conclude whether they come across such situations. If a country is not free from this kind of corruption, the government should come forward to check it with care. Corruption may lead to sufferings such as loss of job and property, poverty, violence, imprisonment and humiliation. It is absolutely bad for society. So honest and wise employees, officers and good citizens will never think of it.

Certainly, there are many good administrators and great statesmen who are committed to the cause of the nation. If the number of such great personalities increases, the shape of the world will assume a different colour, and peace, prosperity and social progress would reign supreme.

The following suggestions may have an important role to play in general administration:

1. Living conditions of citizens, including service holders, may be improved. The task of social transformation may be undertaken. Decent salary may be paid to the employees.

2. Attention may be paid to economy, poverty, food, health, education, etc.

3. Security of life and property and the sovereignty of the country may be kept intact.

4. The unemployment problem enhances poverty; so beware of it.

5. Environmental and pollution problems may be solved.

6. Ample opportunity may be given to citizens to drink deep from the fountains of culture and spiritualism.

7. Moral character, sincerity, efficiency, qualification, etc., of the employee may not be overlooked. Different types of prizes may be given to the best administrators and other employees.

8. Care may be taken to counsel government servants and other employees in the matter of raising their moral turpitude.

9. Attempts may be made to change the hearts of miscreants and prisoners. Counseling centres, morality cells, awareness-building institutions, etc., may be opened.

10. International relationship may be largely improved.

11. Dispute, war, communalism, terrorism and corruption will have no place in society. These points should be seriously viewed.

12. Vigilance Commissions may be made more independent, active, impartial and strong.

13. Through the length and breadth of the country the steed of law carrying justice should gallop to eradicate evil and establish peace and order.

14. Of course, these things are not new and the benevolent governments of different countries are taking an active interest in eradicating corruption. But in the face of such attempts evil is luxuriantly growing in some corners of the world. Let us strenuously work and hope that evil would vanish from society in due course of time. But all of us have to make special efforts at making this world a better place to live in.

CHAPTER X

Our Vision and Conclusion

Global welfare constitutes our vision. The concept of one world has a deep connection with our vision. Wendell Willkie, an American preacher, propagated the concept of one world many years ago. Jawaharlal Nehru strongly supported this concept. We have a vision of establishing a just society where a common approach to the problems of humanity is entertained. As the rapid progress in science and technology has made the world smaller, it is possible to think of a sort of commonness in the way of life of the people. Conflict, hatred, violence and tension are the common features of the world. So they can be unitedly solved.

Now political, social and economic problems have been a menace to some countries. Co-operation between nations can easily solve the problem and establish peace and order in the contemporary world. Justice, equality and fraternity owe their origin to the international outlook, understanding and perfect unity without hypocrisy. The common needs and problems, the basic instincts, the basic principles, security of life and, above all, the proper study of humankind widen our vision to go deep into the subject and the progress of the people of the whole world. Selfishness, corruption and hypocrisy create problems in the way of peace and prosperity of a nation. Terrorism, poverty, disease, religion, intolerance, sex-culture and lack of sex sublimation create problems in nations. Now, this is mainly leading to violence, rape, murder, etc. Let us govern our passions or they will govern us.

Language is a unifying factor. So the international language should be systematically taught in every country. A healthy interaction of the people belonging to different nations, cultures and languages in the common language is much more effective than in any other language. It paves the way to the unity of the world.

Great statesmen and super politicians are the best master of the situations arising from world problems. They should tackle such problems with sympathy, imagination, great vision and elasticity in the choice of means. Some of the leaders and a great many responsible citizens of the democratic world could realise the value of world peace after two World Wars and they came forward to form the UNO, which is now at work to bind the world with a common thread.

Sometimes religious thoughts, fanaticism, superstitions, etc., create problems in the way to world peace. Although different countries might be worshipping gods with different names and shapes, there is every possibility of worshipping one Creator God. This would lead to religious understanding and tolerance. Religions bring peace. It never teaches hatred and bloodshed. Since religion is the guiding force of man, it has to be embraced. The concept of one God can remove conflicts and misunderstandings.

Modern inventions of science and technology would go a long way towards human transformation. Science and religion are not and should not be contradictory to each other. If we carefully handle the task of social transformation, human resource development, etc., we can very well remove poverty, disease and ignorance, which is the pressing need of the hour. All countries should be equal before the eye of law. Some sort of world-reformation in the present world-order should take place. It should begin at home. Some may argue that family is the lowest social unit in the world. So it may be insignificant in the arena of world-order, they argue. No. We should begin at home. Lack of spirituality, irresponsibility of householders, ill-treatment of women, lower status of women, idleness, bad habits, incompatibility, immorality and corruption should vanish from society. The whole thing is a stepping-stone to world peace and order. Marriages between men and women of different countries foster international understanding. Happy homes pave the way to a happy world.

So, reformation of family and neighborhood is very important in the regional, national or international strata. If every citizen or family does not develop, how can the world experience collective development?

Indians uphold the idea of *Vasudheiva Kutumbakam*. It means that the whole world is one family. This idea needs to be translated into action. The 'survival of the fittest' theory should be replaced by the dogma, 'survival of all, the rich and the poor; the high and the low; the wise and the innocent; the fortunate and the unfortunate alike'. 'Live and let live' should be the order of the day.

Our vision embraces three main dimensions: God, humanity and transformation. We will transform children and youths, adults and the old alike, into a super humanity. One of our writers writes: 'Children are the multicoloured flowers and youths are the radiant fruits of God's garden'. Youths possess vigour, vitality, serviceability and magnanimity. So they can very well soar like an eagle and sing the glory of God. International peace does not lie only in the development of economy, science, etc. It lies in giving up arms and ammunition and developing the goodness of heart.

The world is the greatest garden of God; it belongs to Him. We cannot touch anything in it with a view to causing it harm. We must live in this garden in accordance with the Law of the Master. We are a special creation here. God has given us knowledge, wisdom, conscience and freedom. These virtues will enable us to soar high if we use them properly. Blossom where you are!

Conclusion

Now the world-drama of animals and men being unfurled by us is fast coming to an end. The reader may have some questions. Let us take a look at them.

1. Is it possible that good people will come onto the world stage in large numbers? This point has already been discussed.

2. Some countries have been facing serious monetary problems. So what about funds for the execution of the schemes mentioned in this book? We have already illustrated that a country would be rich overnight if only corruption is checked.

3. It is all nothing but "an ineffective angel beating his luminous wings in void." If you do not do anything, you will face a crisis. If you do not perform honestly, you will face serious problems. The answers are with you.

Within a few years the theory mentioned in the foregoing chapters was put into practice; as a result of which people largely began to be good. The election officers of different parts of the world ordered for election of members to various panchayats, councils, assemblies and parliament, beginning from the grass-roots level to the centre. As there were now an overwhelming majority of Super Beings and good people in countries, suitable candidates won elections with flying colours and formed good governments. Now there was not anything bad in the administration. However, the opposition was in existence. The ruling party began to strengthen the opposition so that it could play an important role in guiding the government. Of course, some countries did not readily accept the plans and suggestions made in this book, as men are resistant to change. But this situation (old order) did not adversely affect the main administrative current of the world. Now all the departments are functioning strictly in accordance with the provisions and styles mentioned in 'Aspects of Political Affairs' and 'General Administration'. Education, culture and literature flourished; corruption, crime, hatred, violence, boundary dispute, war, terrorism and communalism lost their identity; poverty, ignorance and disease vanished; improvement in the fields of agriculture, science and technology was marvellous; and problems related to communication, ecology and environment were felt no more. Peace and prosperity lent a special charm to the world.

If winter comes, can spring be far behind? The world lost is regained. People began to feel as if they were in a big, natural garden, full of flowers, fruits, springs, birds, milk and honey. We were born in winter, lived in winter and now by His grace we could see the wonderful spring almost everywhere in the world. We enjoyed the splendour of the spring. Dreams came true.

Spring, spring everywhere,
No more comes the winter.

God came down to see the happy people. He blessed them so that their lives could be even better. But it has already been said earlier that the world can never be free of bad people. Of course, the number of such people is now very small and meagre. So, in no corner of society, are there any problems.

Now the philosophical thoughts of Super Beings are superb, their administrative systems are beneficent, the galloping of the steed of law is colourful and commending, the activities of the citizens are excellent and the transformation is marvellous. God alone is capable of transforming and developing (all round) mankind, and this is exactly what we find here. So the petition! Three cheers to those of the blessed, transformed and cultured people whose life-boats are not running adrift on the turbulent waters of the world-ocean. Yes, peace, prosperity and social and spiritual transformation are achieved only when the vision of the people changes for the better.

Now a vast majority of the people are happy and looking forward to seeing the day of the great judgment— the day on which bad people would be condemned to hell and good people would be exalted to heaven, where "Moakshya" (liberation) waits for them and where supreme happiness governs for all eternity.

So let us worship and adore the Creator and Liberator God and be good and do good to others. All the features mentioned in this book will, we are sure, lead to full social transformation, a new world-order and international peace and understanding.

We must never forget that 'truth alone triumphs'— *Satyameva Jayate*. Only truth should be sought in the spheres of human society, science and religion.

O ye sons of men, how long will ye turn my glory into shame? How long will ye love vanity, and seek after leasing (lies)?

—Psalm 4:2